Las Cruces, New Mexico
1849-1999
Multi-Cultural Crossroads

Gordon Owen
1999

Las Cruces, New Mexico
1849–1999: Multicultural Crossroads
Copyright 1999 by Cultural Society of Mesilla Valley
Second Printing 1999
All rights reserved.

ISBN 1-881325-31-8 cloth
ISBN 1-881325-32-6 paper
Library of Congress
#98-068291

1. New Mexico History; 2. Las Cruces, New Mexico
Territorial History; 3. Las Cruces, New Mexico Statehood
History; 4. Doña Ana, New Mexico History; 5. Mesilla, New
Mexico History

Editing: The Drs. Donna & Carl Eichstaedt

Red Sky Publishing Co., Inc.
Las Cruces, New Mexico 88011

Dedicated With Love
To
My Devoted Wife, Ardis
Stephen, Susan, Daniel, Philip and William

Bio

Gordon R. Owen, Ph. D., is an emeritus professor of Communication Studies at New Mexico State University. He is author of *The Two Alberts* , a blended biography of Albert Fountain and Albert Fall. A native of Ohio, he grew up in southern Indiana. After World War II service in China-Burma-India Theater, he earned degrees at University of Minnesota and a Ph. D. at Purdue University. He taught in Indiana and Arizona public schools for eight years and at New Mexico State University for twenty-seven years. He and his wife Ardis have been married for fifty-two years and have a daughter and four sons, eight grandchildren and a great grandson. His retirement hobby is exploring the mysteries of local history.

Table Of Contents

List of Illustrations .vii, viii
Preface . . . . .ix, x, xi
Foreword . . . . .xiii, xiv, xv
Map xvi

Chapter 1: Pioneering Cultures 1
Chapter 2: Pioneering Communities 15
Chapter 3: Civil War 33
Chapter 4: The Railroad and Stability 48
Chapter 5: Education 70
Chapter 6: Law, Order and Statehood 95
Chapter 7: Water And The Butte 118
Chapter 8: Banking And Growth 129
Chapter 9: Successful Families 149
Chapter 10: The Proving Ground 173
Chapter 11: Renewal 189
Chapter 12: The Fabulous Future 204

Appendices:
1 Doña Ana County Sheriffs 225
2 Mayors of Las Cruces 226
3 Population Statistics - Las Cruces 227
4 New Mexico State University Enrollments 228
5 Town Survey & Recording 1849 229
6 Presidents of N.M.S.U. 230
7 Company A New Mexico National Guard 1916 . .231
8 W.W. II Philippine Fatalities 232
9 Historical Society Hall of Fame 233
Sources 234

Index 238

List of Illustrations

Early Mesilla street scene 27
Lt. Sackett's plotting map 29
Map of 84 block plotting of Las Cruces 31
Main Street (city bakery and Second Class Saloon) 45
1st Doña Ana county courthouse 46
Las Cruces in 1905 50
North Main Street looking north 51
H.H. Brooks, 1st Doña Ana County Agent. 1915 53
Horse races were held on north Alameda Drive each Sunday 55
Dripping Springs Hotel. Organ Mountains. "Old Van Patten's" 57
Las Cruces Santa Fee Depot, 1910 58
Modoc Mine, one of the largest Organ Mt. Operations, 1890's 60
Amador Hotel Interiors, 1916 and 1921 62
First Residence Building, Shalam Colony, 1889 64
W.I.A. Club House on North Reymond 66
Van Patten Home, Dripping Springs, 1897 68
Las Cruces Tennis Club, 1896 68
Alameda Lane, 1897 74
Loretto Academy 76
St. Genevieve's Catholic Church on North Main 77
The Gazebo in the City (Pioneer) Park 80
Pioneer Park 83
The old and new 1910 Mitchell Auto at what became Broadway Motel .84
Hiram Hadley in front of 1st college building (South Ward School)
    1889 86
Cornerstone laying. McFie Hall (Old Main), 1890 88
Old Main, 1st NM College of A&MA Building, 1891 89
Hadley Hall, NM A&MA, built in 1909 92
Y.M.C.A. Building, NMSU 93
Old science building, NMSU, built in 1897 94
Arcadian Club, 1895 99
Col. Albert Jennings Fountain 101
Senator Albert Bacon Fall 103
Henry J. Fountain, age 8 107
Chalk Hill, site of disappearance of Albert & Henry Fountain 109
Sheet Music cover page. Elizabeth Garrett's
    "Oh Fair New Mexico," 1917 111
Ex-President Teddy Roosevelt arrives in Las Cruces via Santa Fe
    Railroad (with R.L. Young) 115
Early work on Elephant Butte Dam, 1911 125
Completed Elephant Butte Dam, 1916 128
Dedication of Doña Ana County Courthouse (1937 or 1938) 142
Dedication of El Molino Grinding Stone, 1st National Bank 144
Doña Ana County Sheriff Felipe Lucero, Deputies Bob Burch and
    Morgan Llewellyn, Church Street 151

Armijo-Gallagher home, north of Loretto Towne Center,
150 E. Lohman 156
Las Cruces Post Office, 1912 Postmaster Capt. Thomas
Branigan and Mrs. Branigan 158
Las Cruces Post Office, 1912 160
The Park Hotel, just north of the City (Pioneer Park) 163
Women's Improvement Association Parade Float, 1944 176
August 30, 1953. Flood on west Picacho Avenue 178
Las Cruces City Hall 186
"The Alameda" Sanatorium (early 1900s) 199

Preface

When Chuck Miles, a member of the Mayor's Sesquicentennial Committee, asked me to consider preparing a short history of the city of Las Cruces, I knew it would be a formidable task. However, as a thirty-six year resident of the city and an emeritus professor from New Mexico State University, the challenge fascinated me. I have devoted my retirement years to the study of local history and was well aware that even if the one hundred fiftieth birthday celebration were not in need of such a publication, a reasonably complete history of the city doesn't exist and should be written.

I therefore set aside other priorities, calmed my wife, who believes a prerequisite to retirement should be a course in how to say NO, and became immersed in several months of research. A major question that had to be answered before embarking on actual writing was how best to structure the historical review. Probably the easiest structural approach, both for writer and readers, would be to organize chronologically, possibly proceeding by decades.

However, it soon became apparent that such an approach might over-simplify the interwoven sequence of influential historic events which transformed a desert crossroads into southern New Mexico's largest city. It is therefore important to recognize the role of such diverse factors as Mexican land grants, border disputes and treaties, the Civil War, floods, arrival of the railroad and telegraph, and the establishment of what became New Mexico State University. To those significant 19th century shaping events must be added the 20th century's building of Elephant Butte Dam and the consequent agricultural greening of the Mesilla Valley, the great depression, World Wars I and II, the establishment of White Sands Proving Ground, and even urban renewal.

Consequently, this publication will to some extent follow a general chronological outline but the greater emphasis will be on those individuals, families, events and forces which have produced the cosmopolitan population and culture of the bustling, bursting-at-the-seams City of the Crosses. One result will be an appearance at times of shifting time frames and some apparent repetition but the complex interaction of multiple ethnic, cultural and personal forces made that necessary.

This task would have proved insurmountable had not the staffs of Branigan Memorial Library and New Mexico State University been so helpful. Austin Hoover, Linda Blazer, Tim Blevins and Cheryl Wilson were most supportive and the photo and archival resources of Rio Grande Historical Collections and Special Collections were invaluable. My sincere and special thanks for major assistance go to long-time residents Margaret Favrot and Representative and Mrs. J. Paul Taylor. The manuscript's volunteer review committee, the 150th anniversary co-chairs, Mayor Ruben Smith and J. J. Martinez, Dr. William Clark, Dr. Laura Gutierrez Spencer, Prof. Austin Hoover and my wife and five children, all contributed selflessly. Many Las Crucens, so numerous I could not possibly credit all of them, have been generous in their assistance to this project. Finally, I especially appreciate the support and friendship of Chuck Miles, Keith Whelpley and his Red Sky Publishing Company, the Doña Ana County Historical Society, and the technical assistance of Fred and Donna Johnson, the Mac Docs. Finally much credit for long hours of proofing, formatting and polishing the final manuscript must go to Donna and Carl Eichstaedt, Susie Whelpley and Gerald Rel, all of Red Sky

Publishing.

James Michener once said "The perfect book has yet to be written." This book does not challenge that generalization, but it must be stated that what errors are contained herein are the author's and not those of any of the many Las Crucens who provided me with assistance and guidance.

Foreword

We humans have traditionally accorded special significance to birthdays and anniversaries. We shower special affectionate attention on childhood and on advanced age birthdays, particularly when a loved one reaches the fiftieth, seventy-fifth or the century mark. It therefore seems reasonable that we should commemorate significant anniversaries of the founding of the communities in which we live.

In much of our nation, communities have existed for two or even three centuries, and in many cases, these were preceded by additional centuries of Indian communities. The skeptic might therefore ask, "Why celebrate a mere one hundred fifty years?" To survive, grow and prosper in the desert Southwest, however, communities must cope with extremes of climatic, terrain and economic adversity. Any city of the American Southwest which reaches its one hundred-fiftieth birthday still prospering, growing and looking to an ever brighter future deserves to pat itself on the back and celebrate. Las Cruces is just such a city, has reached its sesqui-centennial and has committed itself to pause, review and reflect on its past, assess its current status and project its future.

To understand Las Cruces as it approaches this very special anniversary, however, one must acquire a detailed awareness of those events in the past century and a half which have been most influential and formative in shaping the city we see today. More important, for the citizens of this city to learn from past successes and failures, visualize the Las Cruces of the future and actively contribute to the actualization of that vision, we must know who and what have shaped our city and how it has happened.

The two words of this volume's sub-title may comprise the most important factors that led from that day in 1849, when approximately one hundred land-hungry but destitute immigrants gathered in a remote desert area to draw lots. Each was to gain a plot of land in a fledgling village to be called Las Cruces, which we now know was to become a rapidly growing city of seventy-five thousand people.

One of those words is demographic: "Multi-Cultural." It was chosen to remind us that not just three dominant cultures, but many sub-cultures have blended to form the human component of Las Cruces. The other term is geographic: "Crossroads." It suggests that location has exerted a major influence on the fortunes of those multi-cultural Las Crucens. The valley of one of this nation's major north-south rivers, the Rio Grande, provided a natural route for the major land link between Santa Fe and Chihuahua, Mexico, the *Camino Real* (Royal Highway). Finally, the flat terrain of southern New Mexico provided a convenient route for east-west pony express, stage coach, wagon train and, ultimately, rail service.

Thus, the site which became Las Cruces, at a natural ford of the Rio Grande and at a practical resting place for north-south travelers, was visited by native Americans, Spanish colonizers, soldiers, priests, traders, gold seekers, and land-seeking settlers. Consequently, tourism and transportation have played critical roles in the evolution of Las Cruces ever since the first human traveler stopped to rest and prepare to cross the river or traverse many miles of desert.

One hundred fifty years ago, the sensible, the cautious, the fearful, the traditionalist moved on. The adventurous, the hardy, the reckless, the stubborn, the optimistic stayed. Where they stayed has been described as harsh, forbidding, unrelenting, a great, fierce, challenging, canyon-gutting, mesa-muscled land, where everything from cactus to cowman carried a weapon. They not only stayed but they made homes for themselves and future generations. Historian-writer and fifty year Las Crucen Lee Priestley expressed it best when she observed that certain types of personality find in the Mesilla Valley their *querencia*, their spiritual home. This volume attempts to focus on those personalities, their careers, their families and their community.

Rio Grande Valley, New Mexico

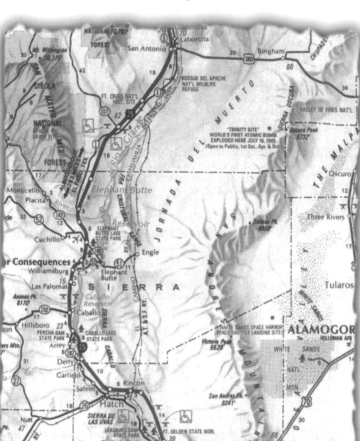

Chapter 1
❧ Pioneering Cultures ❧

The most distinctive physical landmark of the Mesilla Valley is the rugged, jagged, inspiring mountain range which borders the eastern side of the Valley. Dubbed by one of the region's earliest Spanish colonizers *Sierra del Olvido* (Mountains of Oblivion or Forgotten Mountains) and, because of the peak's resemblance to organ pipes, by a later Spanish governor as *Los Organos* (The Organs), this range is a southern extension of the Rocky Mountains. Undergoing uniquely lovely chameleon-like color changes at varying times of day, weather conditions and seasons of the year, the Organs are the primary reason the Mesilla Valley is often referred to as "the land of colorful contrasts." They are considered by Valley residents to be the loveliest mountains of the entire country.

Geologists tell us that some 600 million years ago

what is now southern New Mexico was covered by a large shallow sea. The retreat of that sea, possibly 150 million years ago, also marked in a general sense the disappearance of dinosaurs. Starting more than 40 million years ago, violent volcanic activity produced those distinctive Organ Mountains. Geologists estimate that significant volcanic activity in the Mesilla Valley area ended about 35 million years ago when craters such as Aden Crater and Kilbourne Hole were created on the desert mesa some miles west of the Rio Grande.

During this same period, 30 or more million years ago, subterranean fault zones were created, from which millennia of shifting and sinking of the crust ultimately produced the Rio Grande Valley. From its source in the Colorado Rockies, the river, following the rift or fault line, then ultimately assumed its present course extending from Colorado to the Gulf of Mexico. In the last few centuries of settlement, the seventy miles of river and fertile farm land extending from what now is Caballo Dam to the Texas-New Mexico boundary have come to be known as the *Mesilla* (little table/mesa) Valley.

As much as 20 thousand years ago, the abundance of game and fish and grasses attracted nomadic hunters and gatherers into the Mesilla Valley. In their earliest forays, these bands stopped briefly at what the Spanish later called *parajes* (camp sites). Starting possibly seven thousand years ago, extended drought conditions narrowed the verdant portion of the valley to areas closest to the river and this forced many nomadic tribes to evolve into farming villagers.

From living in brush lean-to shelters, native Americans began by 2000 B.C. to build rock shelters and pit houses with thatched roofs. Such settlements tended to cluster near the rivers. In fact, archeologists have discovered ruins of a village on the west bank of the Rio

Grande just north of Mesilla Dam which, because of the profusion of cat tails, they called *Las Tules*. By 1200 B. C., these villagers were growing corn, necessarily a drought-resistant variety, and soon after, beans and squash.

By 1000 A.D the Mogollons, one sub-culture, had begun to build near their fields above-ground homes, called *jacales*, huts of sticks and mud, roofed with brush. The pithouses then were relegated to storage or ceremonial purposes. In fact, by 1300 A. D., some two-story structures were built, forerunners of the multi-room buildings still found today in Indian villages, called *pueblos*, such as Taos and Acoma.

A combination of drought conditions and the gradual arrival of hostile Athabascan-speaking nomadic tribes had dire consequences for the Pueblo Indians. Raids by these Apaches, moving south from Canada through the intermountain west in 1200 to 1500 A.D. led, by about 1450 A.D., to the dwindling and often the desertion of many of the Pueblo villages, especially those distant from the Rio Grande.

By the 16th century, as the Spanish began to arrive, they met early residents who have been called "Mansos," generally considered to be descendants of Mogollon Pueblos. The name "Manso" supposedly originated when early Spanish colonizers were greeted by the Indians with "*manxo, manxo, micos, micos*". Some historians report the greeting as "*mansos, mansos y amigos* ." Either way, the English meaning was "we are peaceable, we are friends." In fact, maps of some of the earliest Spanish explorers designated what are now the Franklin and Organ mountains as *Sierra de los Mansos* (Mountains of the Mansos). Their language and culture tended to be similar to that of the Tarahumara Indians in Sonora and Chihuahua, Mexico. Arrival of hostile Indians, Spanish explorer/settlers, and American traders over the centuries caused many of the Mansos to settle near the mission church in Juarez. Eventually, many of them joined immigrants from Senecu and Ysleta del Sur to establish Tortugas, still a distinct cultural community on the south side of Las Cruces.

The 15th century decline of the Pueblo Indian presence in the Southwest roughly coincided with the arrival of European explorers. Early in the 16th century, Spanish explorers began to probe the southern coastline of what now is the United States and the Spanish conquerors of Mexico began to cast covetous eyes northward.

One exploratory sea expedition, led by Panfilo de Narvaez set out from Cuba in 1528 to explore Florida. Harassed by Indians in Florida, they moved west along the coast of the Gulf of Mexico until they suffered a shipwreck off what now is Texas. A group of four survivors, led by Alvar Nuñez Cabeza de Vaca, and including a Moorish slave, Estevanico, wandered for seven years from tribe to tribe in Texas. They apparently were at times enslaved by Indian groups but as traders and self-styled medicine men, they survived and gradually trudged westward. The four half-starved ragged stragglers finally arrived at a small village, believed to have been somewhere in what now is southern New Mexico. While they may or may not have traveled as far west as the El Paso area, they certainly must have been the first Europeans to visit New Mexico. Aided by native escorts, the group then traveled south, ultimately arriving at Mexico City in 1535.

Cabeza de Vaca pleased and excited Viceroy Antonio de Mendoza with glowing reports of the gold, silver and turquoise the quartet of wanderers claimed to have seen during their seven-year odyssey. By 1539 the Viceroy was ready to confirm or discount Cabeza's glowing report. He dispatched a Catholic priest, Father Marcos de Niza, to reconnoiter the northern frontier, accompanied by Estevanico, the only member of Cabeza de Vaca's party willing to venture back north.

Upon approaching Indian villages in what is now the Zuni pueblo, Fray Marcos sent Estevanico ahead to scout the village, Hawikuh. When word came to Marcos that the Zunis had killed Estevan, the priest very cautiously approached the cluster of villages which he was sure were the fabled Seven Cities of Cibola. He viewed the pueblos from a distant mesa and in the glow of sunset was positive they were the fabled cities of gold, and so reported to the Viceroy upon his hasty return to Mexico.

Viceroy Mendoza then decided to send a full scale expedition to the northern frontier and selected a close and trusted friend, Francisco Vasquez de Coronado as its leader. The Viceroy and Coronado's wife each contributed what today would amount to a million dollars to the project. As the Spanish prepared to extend their much heralded quest for God, glory and gold northward, Fray Marcos was selected as their guide. The expedition included five other friars, 336 soldiers and close to a thousand Indian allies.

From 1540 to 1542, Coronado's men traveled more than four thousand miles, exploring portions of today's Arizona, including the Grand Canyon, and much of northern New Mexico. They even ventured through the Texas Panhandle and Oklahoma to the plains of Kansas. The search for the seven cities of gold and for the fabled Gran Quivira treasure-filled community, which Indian guides kept insisting was "a little further east," and even for converts to Catholicism failed. Coronado returned to Mexico discredited and discouraged. Consequently,

❧ Pioneering Cultures ❧

Spanish interest in lands to the north waned and for forty years no official northward probes were authorized.

However, the Coronado expedition did pave the way for future colonization of New Mexico by making the region reasonably well known. There also persisted the suspicion that Coronado just had not searched in the right areas for the kind of wealth Cortez had found in Mexico. As Paul Horgan put it, "Coronado's failure was forgotten but his hope was still remembered." In 1581 the Viceroy granted permission to a Fransciscan, Fray Agustin Rodriguez, to venture northward in search of converts. Accompanied by two other Franciscans, eight soldier volunteers under the command of Francisco Sanchez Chamuscado and nineteen Indian servants, they traveled the Rio Grande Valley all the way north to Taos. When the Franciscans decided to stay and build a mission among the Pueblos, the soldiers and one of the friars returned to Mexico.

Concern over the fate of the friars left behind led a friend, Fray Bernardino Beltran, to go searching in 1582 for them. A wealthy merchant, Antonio de Espejo, agreed to finance and lead such an expedition. With two friars, thirteen soldiers and a few Indian servants, they traveled north to the Rio Grande, stopping to rest at the southern edge of the Mesilla Valley. It was here, near the present community of Canutillo, that Espejo's scribe reported seeing Manso Indian villagers living in straw huts.

The Espejo expedition soon learned that the Franciscans they sought had been killed, but they nevertheless embarked on a thirty-five hundred mile unsuccessful gold-seeking exploration of the New Mexico-Arizona region. Heading homeward they encountered hostility from the Pueblos at *Puaray*, north of present day

Albuquerque, and executed sixteen captives. Upon
arrival in Mexico City, however, Espejo gave the hoped
for but exaggerated recital of the potential wealth he had
found to the north. In response, Spanish King Philip
issued a royal decree directing the viceroy to arrange a
contract with some responsible citizen to go, at his own
expense, to settle and pacify the land now known as
New Mexico, with emphasis on conversion of the native
peoples.

In 1590, Gaspar Castaño de Sosa, lieutenant-gover-
nor of Nuevo Leon province in Mexico, set about to
move the entire population of the mining town of
Almaden northward to establish a settlement in New
Mexico. He led 170 potential settlers and a long supply
train up the Pecos river and established a settlement
near the pueblo later called Santo Domingo. Believing
that as lieutenant governor he had the legal right to
establish a new colony, he notified the Viceroy in Mexico
City of his accomplishment. The Viceroy's response was,
however, to send an army detachment to arrest him for
unauthorized colonization. Castaño was tried, convicted
and exiled to China. The decision later was reversed and
Castaño was named governor of the new colony. As he
returned from China, however, he was killed.

Also in 1590. two army captains, Francisco Leyva de
Bonilla and Antonio Gutierrez de Humaña, led another
unauthorized and ill-fated venture into New Mexico, for
which the Spanish government labeled them fugitive
deserters. Later expeditions learned that Bonilla was
killed by Humaña, who in turn was killed by Indians.

Thus, the Spanish had, by 1595, entered New
Mexico at least six times. None had stayed or successfully established a permanent settlement, but King Philip II
and his Mexican viceroy were convinced the time had
now come for settlement. The man chosen to implement

the kingdom's settlement plan was Don Juan de Oñate, who ultimately was governor of the colony and is referred to by some as "Father of New Mexico."

Oñate, born in 1552, was the son of a wealthy Basque owner of silver mines at Zacatecas, Mexico. Starting early in his teens, he had spent nearly twenty years exploring the frontier and fighting the Chichimec Indians. In his late thirties he made a remarkably fortuitous career and family move, marrying a descendant of both Cortez, the conqueror of Mexico, and of Montezuma, the famed Aztec emperor. Learning of the Spanish government's commitment to authorizing a colonizing and gold seeking expedition to the north, Oñate was ready to invest a fortune in leading such a venture.

In 1595, Oñate contracted with the viceroy to finance and command a settlement expedition, organize it as a kingdom within the empire, and serve as its captain-general and governor. After a three year delay dealing with bureaucratic red tape and the intrigues of envious rivals, he started north in 1598. His expedition consisted of nearly 500 aspiring colonists, nearly 200 fully equipped soldiers, 130 families, 8 Franciscan friars, a number of Indian allies, and 7,000 head of livestock, (horses, mules, oxen, cattle, sheep, goats and pigs). They utilized 83 *carretas* (long narrow carts with bodies of willows lashed together and wheels of crosscuts of huge trees) to transport assorted supplies such as seeds, grains, tools and weapons, as well as products to trade with the Indians.

After a grueling journey through northern Mexico, on April 20, 1598, the three mile long caravan reached the south bank of the Rio Grande. By April 30, the province of New Mexico was formally proclaimed. Governor Oñate stated: "I take possession, once, twice, and thrice, and all the times I can and must, of the . . .

lands of the Rio del Norte, without exception whatsoever." A great ecclesiastical and secular celebration then began. Oñate's scribe reported it included "a sermon, a great salute and rejoicing and, in the afternoon, a comedy." (Although they were not actually at the present site of El Paso, it is this celebration to which El Pasoans refer as "the first Thanksgiving in the New World.")

Traveling north, they were met by friendly Manso Indians who brought them supplies and helped find a ford of the Rio Grande. On May 5, the Oñate caravan crossed the river and headed north along the west foothills of the Organ Mountains, east of the present site of Las Cruces. During the seventeen day journey to the entrance of the desolate *Jornada del Muerto* (Journey of the Dead), a child had died. Then, sixty year old Pedro Robledo was, according to one report, a drowning victim. His burial site marked what travelers for years referred to as the *Paraje de Robledo* (Robledo camp site) and a nearby 5,876 foot high mountain is known as Robledo Mountain.

Good fortune helped the caravan survive a severe water shortage on the arid *Jornada*. It was noticed that one of the pack of dogs which trailed the expedition appeared with muddy paws. Thirsty soldiers hopefully followed the dog and, in fact, did discover a water source, which they named the spring of *Perrillo* (Little Dog).

After nearly six months on the *Camino Real*, the Oñate caravan had extended the Royal Road 1600 miles from Mexico City to Santa Fe. This made it the oldest and longest continuously traveled highway in North America. The colonizers also established and named thirty individual *parajes* (campsites) along the way. They settled near the pueblo of San Juan, north of present day Santa Fe, in the Rio Grande Valley. Assisted by some fifteen hundred Indians, they organized their village, prepared their fields for the following spring and built a church.

Governor Oñate then called together leaders of all the pueblos and announced the Indian villages would ultimately be divided among the eight friars, to whom the Indians would be expected to offer allegiance, support and labor. The governor then set about organizing the new province according to the Spanish blueprint, establishing missions, military *presidios* (fortifications) and *estancias* (large family operated ranches, with adjacent communal grazing lands) in each village.

Once the work on the new capital city, to be called San Gabriel, was well under way and settlers were getting established, Oñate began the search for mineral riches. He led eighty men east down the Canadian River, across Oklahoma, but failed, as had Coronado, to find the fabled Quivira. He then headed west with thirty men, reaching the Colorado River and followed it down to the Gulf of California, but searches for gold or silver were futile. These failures plus discord and violence between Spanish settlers and Indians led to discontent among some of the colonists.

Late in their first fall at San Gabriel, Governor Oñate sent his nephew and second-in-command, Juan de Zaldivar, to explore lands to the west. After camping overnight below Acoma pueblo's Sky City, the Zaldivar squad accepted the Acomans' invitation to climb to the mesa top and visit in their homes. Once divided, the Spanish were subjected to a surprise assault which left Zaldivar and ten of his men dead. In retaliation, Oñate rushed an armed force to Acoma and ordered an assault on the pueblo which resulted in the death of many Acomans and the mutilation or enslavement of the survivors. News of the Acoman incident and continuing reports of colonist discontent led the Spanish crown to suspend Oñate from the governor's office and even to consider giving up on the New Mexican venture.

However, the Franciscan friars reported good Indian response to their mission work, claiming at least eight thousand conversions. So, a king who had come to regard the Indians as not only souls to be saved but as a ready labor force was not about to abandon New Mexico. In fact, for the next three quarters of a century, the Hispanic settlers, soldiers and priests, never numbering more than three thousand souls, so successfully achieved their labor and proselytizing goals that an extremely important result for the future of New Mexico was this period's blending of culture and mingling of blood.

Oñate, now the deposed governor, left New Mexico in late 1609, having suffered great personal financial loss. In 1614 he was tried for colonial mismanagement, convicted, fined and permanently exiled from New Mexico. However, his Zacatecan mines soon restored his fortune and after a 1621 trip to Spain and an audience with the king, Oñate's fine was reimbursed, his good name was restored and he was named royal inspector of all Spanish mines.

Oñate may have been viewed as a failure in the first decade of the 17th century but a major contribution to posterity was his establishment of permanent settlements and regular commerce between Santa Fe (and points north) and Chihuahua (and points south). Beginning in 1619, every three years a thirty-two wagon train, flying royal banners, sanctioned by the church and the King's Viceroy, made the round trip from Mexico City to Santa Fe. Escorted by priests and soldiers and driving herds of animals, these caravans traversed the route blazed by Oñate in 1598, which they now called the *Camino Real de*

❀ Pioneering Cultures ❀

Tierra Adentro (Royal Road of the Interior Lands).

The Mesilla Valley became a regularly visited resting place at *parajes* where Doña Ana, Brazito and Cañutillo ultimately were to be located. North-bound travelers prepared for the rigors of the arid, almost waterless *Jornada del Muerto* and south-bound caravans stopped for rest and recuperation after surviving the *Jornada*. North-bound caravans brought supplies to the Franciscan friars and their missions and finished goods to Santa Fe merchants. As trade developed, they returned south with blankets, piñon nuts, hides, sheep and even Indian slaves. In time it also became a major supply route between mines in southern Colorado and those in Chihuahua.

During the seventeenth century, the Spanish kings and their Mexican viceroys jealously guarded this trade route. They saw New Mexico as their last barrier against French and English colonization. To protect their prospering trade monopoly and discourage French or English incursions, they forbade any trade with foreigners. Vatican church leaders also were encouraged by optimistic reports from their friars regarding the number of converts.

Nevertheless, Spain nearly lost its colonial source of trade wealth and native converts as conditions steadily worsened in their *Nuevo Mexico*. Seventy-five years after Oñate began colonization, the colony contained only thirty-five hundred non-Indians, many of them feeling only tenuous loyalty to the government and looking for the first opportunity to return to Mexico. Nearly half the populace, Indian and non-Indian, were nearing drought-caused starvation. At Humañas Pueblo alone, now called Gran Quivira, 450 Indians starved to death. Epidemics such as smallpox killed thousands of Indians.

Most ominous was a rising surge of Indian rage over

the efforts of the Franciscans and the government to eradicate all vestiges of Indian religion. Rain making ceremonies were banned and medicine men were imprisoned, whipped and even hanged. Despite their long-standing history of each village fiercely defending its independence, such galling repression had the effect of uniting the traditionally independent Indian population. Meanwhile, the Spanish-appointed governor had only 170 trained soldiers to defend the entire colony.

When Pueblos from northern villages confronted Governor Treviño, he ordered the release of more than forty imprisoned medicine men. One of those men, Pope' (Popay), seething with anger over his beatings, spent the next five years preparing his Pueblo compatriots to unite in rebellion against their Spanish persecutors. On August 10, 1680, full scale rebellion began. After attacking missions and killing friars in outlying communities, the Pueblo warriors converged on Santa Fe and laid siege to the Governor's Palace.

The new Governor, Antonio de Otermin, held out for nine days, hoping that a supply train, organized by Father Francisco de Ayeta, superior of the colony's Fransciscans, might arrive. However, Father Ayeta was in fact waiting in El Paso for Rio Grande flood waters to recede. He now knew that as many as four hundred colonists and more than twenty priests had died and he also believed Indian claims, which proved false, that all Spanish south of Santa Fe had been either slain or captured. Accepting the inevitable, Governor Otermin deserted Santa Fe and led his refugees down the Rio Grande toward the Mesilla Valley and ultimately El Paso. The evacuation did result in founding several communities such as *Paso del Norte* (Juarez) and the forerunner of Tortugas, but the short term consequence of the Pueblo Revolt was that Spain had for the first time in history lost a complete province to its native people.

Governor Otermin attempted to retake the colony in late 1681 but after sacking and burning three villages, he was confronted by an Indian army south of Santa Fe and returned to El Paso. Ten years later, the Spanish crown appointed a soldier of noble blood, Don Diego de Vargas, to serve as governor-in-exile and plan an attempt at reconquest. In 1692, de Vargas, accompanied by 200 soldiers and a group of priests, was astonishingly successful in peacefully reconquering the entire colony. Pope' and other revolt leaders had died so de Vargas successfully employed a divide and conquer approach, winning over each pueblo in turn, as the unity of 1680 had dissolved. The reconquerer then triumphantly returned to El Paso for fresh supplies and personnel.

In 1693, de Vargas again marched north, this time with fewer soldiers but with seventy prospective settler families and eighteen friars. To his dismay, he found many pueblos had reneged on their previous year's peaceful acceptance of his rule. He had to take Santa Fe and other pueblos by storm and even weathered a mini-revolt in 1696. However, by 1700 the reconquest was virtually complete. The Spanish had learned the value of compromise and the Pueblos had accepted that their tradition of total independence of each pueblo was lost forever, and that they too must compromise. It is estimated that there were as many as fifty thousand Indians in ninety pueblos in the colony in the early 1600s but a century later war, diseases such as smallpox and measles, famine and Apache attacks left no more than fourteen thousand survivors in nineteen villages.

Chapter 2
❦ Pioneering Communities ❦

By 1700, with Spanish-Pueblo Indian hostilities relatively settled, profitable *Camino Real* trade resumed. However, a new threat soon intensified. Spanish traders and colonizers had unwittingly exacerbated their own problem by introducing fine horses to the desert country. By the 1600s bands of nomadic Athabascans had moved in from the north. They soon were raiding Pueblo and Spanish villages with horses being a prized target. Stolen or traded horses became "engines of war" for the Apaches and Navajos. Raiding parties were an especially serious threat to traders traversing the *Camino Real* and trade at times ground nearly to a halt.

The Spanish crown and its viceroys had established two *presidios* (garrisons) of regular troops, at El Paso (Juarez) and at Santa Fe. But the king was so preoccupied with troubles in Europe and the incursions of the French and English into Spanish territory elsewhere in America that he neglected New Mexico. In the 1720s, the Santa Fe *presidio* had a complement of only eighty men and maintenance of some semblance of order would have been impossible without the assistance of citizen militia, forerunner of the National Guard, and Pueblo Indian auxiliaries.

Even cities fell prey to raiding parties. Comanche warriors attacked Albuquerque in 1774, driving off the town's entire herd of horses and a huge flock of sheep. In 1775, forty-one settlers of New Mexico were killed in raids by Apaches, Navajos and Comanches. The entire colony felt itself under a state of siege. However, the tide began to turn when the crown and its viceroys agreed to send additional troops into New Mexico and appointed Don Juan Bautista de Anza as governor. Leading a force of six hundred men, he fought and defeated the Comanches in southern Colorado in 1779. He then negotiated a treaty with them which restored lasting peace to eastern New Mexico for the next hundred years. Comanches even joined New Mexico forces in their attempts to combat Apache and Navajo raiders.

The Spanish were increasingly apprehensive over the fact that the Atlantic seaboard colonies not only had won their independence from the English but had successfully organized a new national government. Westward expansion of the U. S. already had begun and the Spanish strategy of returning Louisiana to France soon backfired. Napoleon forgot or ignored his promise that France would never let that territory be handed over to a third power and, in 1803, sold the entire Louisiana Territory to the United States.

Equally worrisome was the 1806-07 arrival of an American expedition led by young Lt. Zebulon Pike.

Mounted Spanish troops arrested Pike and his men, seized his notes and maps and eventually transported all the Americans to Chihuahua and thence back to Louisiana. However, the young explorer prepared a report from memory and its publication in 1810 advertised the trade potential if routes to New Mexico could be developed.

The year 1810 proved a watershed year for Spain in the Rio Grande Valley. After nearly a century of warfare, the Spanish government agreed to a treaty which granted the Mescalero Apaches land in the Sacramento Mountains and also promised them rations, on condition that raiding of wagon trains traversing the Rio Grande Valley be reduced or eliminated. Relative peace then prevailed for twenty-five years and vigorous *Camino Real* trade soon resumed. However, 1810 also saw the same desire for independence, which had sparked the American Revolution in 1776 and the bloody French revolution in 1789, spread to Spain's Mexican colony.

Father Miguel Hidalgo y Costilla convinced his parishioners at the town of Dolores, northwest of Mexico City, that the time had come to declare independence from Spain. His proclamation of liberty, the *grito de Dolores* (shout from Dolores) on September 16, 1810, aroused a tremendous widespread response and Mexico's war for independence began. The Mexican people still commemorate their Independence Day on each sixteenth of September. After more than ten years of sporadic violence, Spain granted Mexico its independence in 1821.

One of the fledgling Mexican nation's first acts was to lift centuries old trade barriers against "foreigners." Within a year, traders from Independence, Missouri, were arriving in Santa Fe with finished goods, which they traded for gold, silver and furs. William Becknell, a famed Indian fighter, had journeyed from Missouri to

Santa Fe in 1821 with a pack train loaded with goods which sold at a sizable profit. He returned the next year with twenty-one men and three wagon loads of goods. Upon returning to Missouri and, for the second year, displaying his impressive profits, the flood gates to western trade were opened. His pioneering feat led historians to call Becknell the "Father of the Santa Fe Trail." Traders such as Josiah Gregg soon were buying goods in Santa Fe and taking or shipping them south on the *Camino Real* to Chihuahua, Durango and Mexico City. Settlements such as El Paso del Norte (Juarez), with an 1840 population of nearly 4,000 people, Socorro and Ysleta soon were booming. Members of New Mexico's upper or *rico* class, exempt from excise taxes because of Mexican citizenship, also entered the trade. Prominent among them was Gov. Manuel Armijo. They annually picked up clothing and manufactured goods in Missouri and freighted them back to Santa Fe, Albuquerque and even Chihuahua. In the first years after Mexican independence, relations were so friendly that the Mexican and U. S. government cooperated in providing military escorts for the trading caravans.

Not only did the newly independent Mexican government open the borders of its New Mexico province to American traders but it also began to offer generous grants of Rio Grande Valley land to land-hungry Mexicans. Overcrowding in the El Paso-Juarez area resulted in adjacent Rio Grande valley land becoming scarce. However, land a few miles north was fertile and available and the Mexican government wanted it settled. Any group of at least 100 individuals who committed to establishing a community on the *cedula* (grant) could apply.

Mexican interest in the Mesilla Valley actually led to settlement attempts even before the 1810-1821 revolution. Juan Garcia de Noriega not only had established holdings near Brazito, thirty miles north of El Paso del Norte, in 1805, but managed for a time to maintain peaceful relations with the Apaches. However, his heirs were run out by the Indians. In 1822, John G. Heath, a friend of one of the best known leaders of early Texas settlement, Stephen F. Austin, applied for and was granted land in the same general area near present day Brazito. Settlement by thirty Catholic families began in 1823 but when the government of Mexican President Augustin de Iturbide was overthrown, no protection was available, and the Apaches also forced those pioneers back to El Paso.

In 1839 Don Jose Maria Costales and 116 settlers from Juarez petitioned for a grant fifteen miles or so north of the aborted Brazito site. The site selected had been known as the Doña Ana *paraje* to travelers for more than two centuries. Various folk tales explain the place name Doña Ana. A legendary woman, widely known but remembered simply as Doña Ana, was reported to have operated a large ranch in the area in the seventeenth century and to have been outstanding for her charity and good deeds. She supposedly had extensive orchards, vineyards, fields of corn, and flocks of sheep.

Another legend reported that Ana, the daughter of a Spanish army officer, had been carried off by Apaches and never seen again, and the site of her kidnapping was named in her memory. A 1693 letter to the Mexican viceroy referred to a sheep ranch of Doña Ana Maria Niña de Cordoba. Still another explanation reports that a child named Doña Ana was buried at a site marked by a wooden cross near present day Doña Ana in 1798. Possibly the most documented legend reported that Ana Robledo, grand-daughter of the Pedro Robledo who had been the first adult fatality in New Mexico of Oñate's 1598 expedition, was a member of the band of refugees who fled south from Santa Fe during the 1680 Pueblo Revolt. When she viewed the site of her grandfather's death and the mountain which consequently bore his name, she was so anguished that she died and was buried near the present day village. There even was a tale that while the original group of land seekers had tarried in El Paso, one of them had promised a lady friend, with whom he had an informal professional relationship, to name the new settlement for her.

A tract of more than 35, 000 acres was certified in 1840 as the Doña Ana Bend Colony grant, on condition that a church, priest's house and public buildings be constructed. It developed, however, that the original petitioners were too impoverished to undertake the move north until January of 1843. Because of fear of Apache attacks, only thirty-three of the original 116 petitioners continued to be interested in the grant in 1843 and even they requested another one month extension.

By February, 1843, Bernabe Montoya led the thirty-three to the area and undertook digging the first *acequia* (irrigation ditch). However, only eighteen actually worked on the *acequia*. Because of continuing fear of Apaches and the lack of provisions, some of those settlers soon abandoned the project, leaving only fourteen hardy, courageous souls to battle the tangled growth of yucca, mesquite, tornillo, cactus and cottonwood. When they requested troop protection and additional laborers from the Mexican government the viceroy, eager to see the settlement succeed, sent Gen. Mauricio Ugarte, military commander of the Juarez presidio, to investigate.

Upon his arrival, only four settlers, Pablo Melendres, original grant applicant Jose Costales, Geronimo Lujan and Jose Bernal met the general and his troops. The others were hiding in the brush because they had no clothing. The general left uniforms for the naked settlers, gave them their first livestock, arranged a tenuous truce with the Mescalero Apaches, and carried to the governor their appeals for protection, exemption from taxes and help with ditch digging.

The Chihuahuan governor responded that he could not exempt them from taxes or provide ditch diggers, but he did send a seven man detachment to protect them. By April, 1843, the settlers, employing the crudest of tools, completed the *acequia* in time for spring planting. The *acequia madre* (primary canal) was considered community property, usable by all settlers who obeyed the rules and helped maintain the ditch.

By January of the next year, 1844, the village had forty-seven families and twenty-two single men, or a total population of 261. Construction had begun on the required church and parish house and, for defensive purposes, the village was built around the traditional plaza. The village of Doña Ana had been successfully founded. The Mexican government appointed Pablo Melendres *alcalde* (mayor/justice of the peace) and Jose Maria Costales as his alternate. In January, 1846, Mexican land officials authorized *Alcalde* Melendres to issue documents of title to Doña Ana land, so long as the original fourteen settlers got first choice. Although the community was growing rapidly, it still was a typical tranquil rural village, as evidenced by one legend of the day which claimed that Doña Ana was so blessed it even had a "watch rooster". which crowed only when danger lurked in the village plaza.

Peaceful relations between Mexico and the United States were soon to be disrupted, however. Several factors led to the United State Congress' declaration of war on Mexico in 1846. The primary motivations were land

hunger and President Polk's "manifest destiny" policy of
satisfying that hunger by extending United States territory from coast to coast. This, combined with U.S.
annexation of Texas in 1845, the ignoring of Mexican
claims to part of that territory, and the unpaid claims
owed by Mexico to U. S. citizens, led to the war declaration.

Mexico still was smarting over its recent loss of
Texas and its leaders were well aware that the Republic
of Texas president, Mirabeau B. Lamar had in 1841 sent
an armed body of soldiers and traders marching toward
Santa Fe. They were easily defeated and sent to prison
in Mexico but the Mexican and New Mexican leaders
regarded the Texas adventure as an armed invasion. In
late 1844, the Mexican government even briefly sus-
pended all business activity. Mexico also became increasingly suspicious of the fur trading mountain men who
considered Taos their headquarters. The governor soon
was ordered to ban fur trapping by anyone but
Mexicans.

When a U.S. offer to purchase the Southwest territories was spurned by Mexico, President Polk looked for a
pretext to seize the coveted territory. Mexican soldiers
crossing the Rio Grande and engaging in an armed skirmish with American troops provided the justification he
needed. Polk went before Congress and announced that
a state of war existed.

Col. Stephen Watts Kearny was named to lead a
major military expedition to the Southwest. In addition
to three hundred army regulars, he recruited thirteen
hundred midwestern volunteers who soon were marching down the Santa Fe Trail. Kearny's troops captured
the village of Las Vegas and then New Mexico's capital
city, Santa Fe, without firing a shot.

Kearny, by then promoted to the rank of General,

was ordered to proceed on to California. However, he
devoted six weeks to reassuring New Mexicans of his
country's desire to make the transition from Mexican to
United States rule as peaceable as possible. Lawyers
from the ranks of his army helped create a set of basic
laws, later called the Kearny Code. Civil officials were
appointed to administer the territory and, to protect
Santa Fe, construction began on Fort Marcy.

As General Kearny moved on west with the bulk of
his army, military command in New Mexico was left in
the hands of Col. Alexander Doniphan. Leaving a garrison under Col. Sterling Price to protect Santa Fe,
Doniphan headed south down the Rio Grande Valley
with 300 mounted and 550 infantry troopers, most of
them untrained and relatively undisciplined Missouri
farm boys. Responding to news of Navajo raids on area
ranches, Doniphan sent his foot soldiers south toward
Doña Ana while he led the mounted men to seek peace
with the Navajos. When Doniphan's troop rejoined the
main body of Missourians, he brought with him a
Navajo promise of peace, then started his 850 man force
southward toward Doña Ana.

These Missourians were described as "free style" soldiers. The line of march often stretched for miles, at one
time nearly one hundred miles. Parties of traders, traveling with the column for protection, were interspersed
with troopers and, since most of the troopers had dis-
carded all or part of their uniforms, traders and troopers
were indistinguishable. As to military discipline, one
observer stated "the greatest irregularities constantly
took place." Yet they proved themselves great fighters.

Upon arriving at Doña Ana, the colonel decided the
village was an ideal spot to rest his troops in preparation
for a push on into Mexico. Doña Ana's pioneer settlers
were beginning to harvest their first bumper crops and

for several weeks provided, as best they could, food and lodging for the Missourians.

Refreshed and somewhat re-supplied, the Doniphan army headed on south and by Christmas Day, 1846, they were setting up camp at Brazito, a few miles south of present day Las Cruces. When a cloud of dust to the south signalled the approach of what proved to be a thousand man Mexican army force, the Missourians quickly prepared to do battle. Approach of the enemy caught Doniphan and his officers engaged in a card game to decide ownership of a recently captured horse. The colonel is said to have shouted: "Boys, I hold an invincible hand, but I'll be damned if I don't have to play it out in steel."

The Missourians' sharp shooting quickly repelled the invasion, with the Mexicans suffering a number of casualties. This proved to be the only battle of the Mexican war fought on New Mexican soil. Doniphan's troops marched triumphantly on to win other victories and capture Chihuahua City. After moving eastward back to the Rio Grande, they traveled by boat either across the river or down the river to the Gulf of Mexico, back to Texas and on to the Midwest. They thus completed one of the most remarkable campaigns in military history, traveling nearly 5,000 miles with limited support or direction from Washington, foraging for subsistence as they went.

In the last months of 1847, peace negotiations between the U. S. and Mexico took place sporadically, interspersed with outbreaks of renewed fighting. In December of 1847, the commanding officer of U.S. troops still in New Mexico, Col. Sterling Price, called a citizens' convention to organize a territorial government. Once accomplished, this seemed to constitute de facto annexation of New Mexico as a territory of the United States, even before formal treaty negotiations could be completed.

It also meant that for nearly sixty-five years, the federal government would appoint top territorial officers such as governor, territorial secretary, supreme court justices, surveyor general, revenue collector, U. S. attorneys and marshals and land office personnel. These appointments often were considered rewards for political favors or a convenient method of removing a rival politician to the desert southwest. Territories were authorized to elect a delegate to the U.S. House of Representatives, but that delegate had no vote and could speak in open session only with consent of the Speaker of the House. Territorial status also called for each county to elect a probate judge, sometimes called prefect, who usually functioned as legislative, executive and judicial officer. In turn, each county was divided into precincts and each precinct elected an *alcalde*.

In February, 1848, however, the Treaty of Guadalupe Hidalgo was signed, formally ending the Mexican War, guaranteeing land grants and insuring New Mexico territorial status. The U. S. negotiator agreed to pay fifteen million dollars for annexation of all of New Mexico and all of California above a line just north of the 32nd parallel. He also agreed to pay the claims of U. S. citizens against Mexico. The Treaty was ratified by the United States in March and by Mexico in May, 1848.

The end of the war had a significant impact on the now growing village of Doña Ana. The Guadalupe Hidalgo treaty ceded all land east of the Rio Grande, including the Doña Ana Bend Colony Grant to the United States. Doña Ana already was, in 1849 terms, becoming overcrowded. Not only were U. S. troops garrisoned there but Texas veterans swarmed in. The Texans claimed the "head right" to undeeded land promised them. This resulted from a secret provision in the 1836 Texas-Mexico treaty ending Texas' war to gain independence from Mexico and signed by the Republic of Texas and Mexican president Santa Anna. Occasional gold seekers who chose the Mesilla Valley rather than continuing the trek to the California gold fields and even Missourians who returned to the Valley after discharge from the Doniphan campaign added to the impression that the village was bursting at the seams.

At this time, land west of the Rio Grande and south of the Gila River was still Mexican territory. Led by Father Ramon Ortiz and El Pasoan Don Rafael Ruelas, and assisted by the Mexican government, more than sixty Doña Ana families decided they preferred Mexican to United States rule. In 1850 they settled on a *mesita* (small hill) on the Mexican west side of the river, and thus the town of Mesilla was born. Initial growth was slow, but there soon was a cluster of adobe houses and, of course, a church. The first place of worship was a *jacal*, vertical poles in a ground trench, laced together, covered with a mud plaster and a roof of dirt, supported by *vigas* and *latillas* (large and small beams).

However, growth soon accelerated. After a revolution in Mexico, a new land commissioner divided the Mesilla grant, designating the southern portion the Santo Tomas de Yturbide Colony. The northern or Mesilla grant of 21,628 acres was to be democratically administered, with an elected council, mayor and justice of the peace. Ruelas was elected *alcalde* and by 1852, when the Mesilla Civil Colony Land Grant was officially awarded, Mesilla counted at least 700 settlers.

That same year, the territorial legislature designated the entire stretch of what now is the southern third of New Mexico and Arizona, extending 800 miles from Texas to the Colorado River, as Doña Ana County and named Mesilla the county seat. It soon became the mercantile and trade center of the Valley. Additional growth also had resulted from the opening of Fort Fillmore, south of Mesilla, in 1851.

The territorial legislature understood the potential of the newly acquired southern region and in 1852 even mandated annual fairs at Mesilla, Doña Ana and Las Cruces and, to encourage commercial development, exempted the county from taxes. Merchants like Reynolds and Griggs, Lesinsky, Freudenthal, Hayward and McGrory, Bull, Barela and Ochoa were doing well. In 1851, a rudimentary structure was built to house San Albino Catholic Church. A permanent sanctuary soon was constructed on the present Plaza site and the present San Albino sanctuary was built in 1906. Mesilla held fiestas, dances, fairs, and even bull fights, with elevated box seats on the plaza facing the church. By 1856-57, the legislature repealed the tax sabbatical and a spe-

Early Mesilla street scene.

cial legislative act in 1878 incorporated Mesilla.

Meanwhile, Doña Ana alcalde Don Pablo Melendres' was seeking another solution to the over-crowding of his village. At the urging of his constituents, in the spring of 1849 he petitioned the United States troops stationed in Doña Ana to assist in surveying and laying out a new town site a few miles south of Doña Ana. The man to whom he was referred was 2nd Lieutenant Delos Bennett Sackett.

Lieutenant Sackett was an 1840 graduate of West Point who had been decorated for meritorious service in the battles of Palo Alto and Resaca de la Palma in the Mexican War. In fact, one biography suggested that dur-ing the Resaca battle Sackett had three horses shot from under him in rapid succession but escaped serious injury and continued fighting. His career was ultimately to win him promotions to the position of Inspector General of the United States Army.

In the summer of 1848, Co. H, 1st Dragoons, eighty-seven strong, were ordered from Ft. Gibson, Indian Territory (Oklahoma), to border duty at Doña Ana, the only real settlement between El Paso and Socorro. Their primary assignment was to protect the small valley com-munities from Apache raids.

Alcalde Melendres requested that Sackett lay out a town "in American fashion," so the lieutenant selected a detail of five men to assist him. The men were limited to the most rudimentary surveying equipment. Legend has it that the primary instrument was a rawhide rope or lar-iat, the length of which varied depending on how dry or wet it was.

Upon arriving at the designated site, the army detail found about one hundred twenty hardy souls already liv-ing in brush huts on the ground where the plaza was to be. In retrospect, it is clear the lieutenant and his men

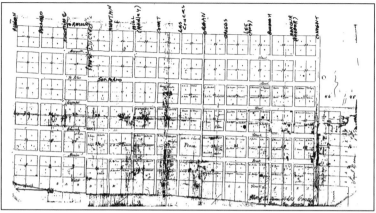

Lt. Sackett's platting map.

did a remarkable job of implementing Don Melendres' request. In addition to a block designated for the plaza and church, eighty four blocks were laid out, each consisting of four lots. Provision was made for wide north-south streets, now named Water (nearest the acequia which initially bound the site on the west,) Main and Church. The other north-south streets were to be Campo, St. Peter (later San Pedro), Mesquite and Tornillo.

In what was to be the anticipated center of the town, between Water and Church Street, fifteen blocks were laid out north to south from a block north of present-day Picacho south to two blocks south of present day Lohman. Between Blocks 22 and 23 was the plaza/church block upon which a simple church structure, forerunner of St. Genevieves, had been erected by1850. (It should be noted, however, that later maps of the platting show the plaza/church block as actually being block #23.) One block, #53, between Campo and San Pedro, was designated for the burial ground (camposanto), which explains the street name, Campo. Proceeding eastward, fifteen blocks also were laid out north to south between Church and Campo, and thirteen blocks each between Campo, San Pedro, Mesquite and Tornillo.

Once Lieutenant Sackett's task was completed, heads of families of the 120 pre-survey residents gathered near the plaza/church site and drew *suertes* (numbers) from a hat for their home sites. Names appearing on the original plat include Trujillo, Bull, Barrio, Campbell, Cuniffe, Lujan, Alderete, Woodhouse, Apodaca, Lucero, Jones, Lara, Armijo, Ochoa, Patton, Miller, Bean, Samaniego, Bernal, Cordova, Barela, Sedillo, Medina, Avalos, Marshall, Calderon, Montoya, Sedillo and Alvarez. (A more complete list is found in Appendix 5 of this volume.) Initially, only 37 blocks plus the church/plaza and cemetery blocks were allocated. Most of the blocks east of Campo and those north of present day Lucero were at this time unclaimed.

Despite Sackett's efforts, or because of the fluctuating lengths of rawhide ropes, some streets were crooked, houses often crowded the street and left what in some cases resembled a maze rather than a planned community. Mud for the largely adobe houses often came from digging holes in the streets. At one point, Judge Richard Campbell ordered people not only to stop making adobes on Main Street but also to fill in the holes already there. Wood was used only for door and window frames plus roof vigas and the pioneers often had to travel to the mountains for timber.

There are multiple theories as to the source of the name of the new town, Las Cruces, or "the crosses." One claimed that in the 18th century a group including a bishop, a priest, a Mexican army colonel and a captain, four trappers and four choir boys were attacked near the Rio Grande and only one boy survived. Crosses were erected and the area came to be known as *El Pueblo del*

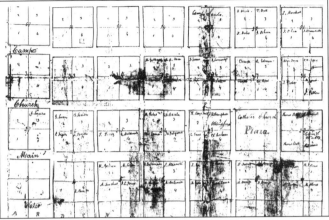

Map of first twenty-eight settled blocks in Las Cruces town site.

Jardin de Las Cruces (City of the Garden of Crosses).
Another theory claimed that brush along the river provided such cover for the Apaches that there were several
small clusters of crosses, marking each massacre, scattered around the river bank. Another story was that in
1830 a group of forty or more travelers from Taos were
slaughtered, resulting in a "forest of crosses."

Still another claim was that a party of troops of New
Mexico's Governor Manuel Armijo was attacked at a
ford in the river in the late 1820s, resulting in fourteen
fatalities, marked by a single cross. That theory may be
most defensible because Susan Magoffin, possibly the
first Anglo woman to travel the Santa Fe and Camino
Real Trails with her trader family, reported seeing in
February 1847, "a hillock of stone and a solitary white
cross."

Still another perspective suggested by some is a lin-
guistic one. The Spanish word for "cross" is *cruz* and the
Spanish word *cruce* means "crossing" or "crossroad". This
very well could mean that none of the white cross expla-
nations for the name Las Cruces is valid and that Las
Cruces is, in fact, a Spanish name for crossing or cross-

road. Whether one or all of these theories is the most accurate "name explanation", it seems reasonable to conclude that the proximity of a Rio Grande ford to Apache raiding areas produced numerous casualties and crosses and thus the "Garden of the Crosses." It also is clear that the crosses served as a landmark for travelers, marking a crossroad and a place to cross the Rio Grande.

Chapter 3
❦ Civil War ❦

The decade of the 1850s was one of growth in all three Mesilla Valley fledgling communities, Doña Ana, Mesilla and Las Cruces, stemming primarily from developing trade. The area had indeed become a major crossroads for north-south and east-west traders, travelers and gold seekers. Fort Fillmore had been established in 1851, providing some promise of safe passage for all those risking travel through Apache territories. By 1850, Las Cruces already had grown to 600 hardy souls and before long, Mesilla had an estimated population of 3,000, making it the largest town and trade center between San Antonio and San Diego. This may have been that town's historic peak of population, as one group of settlers moved north to the village of Picacho in 1854 and in its early years, the Mesilla area was decimated by malaria.

Mesilla Valley merchants received most goods from St. Louis via Santa Fe. In 1859, 1,532 wagons, each carrying 5,500 pounds, passed through the town of Council Grove, Kansas, heading west on the Santa Fe Trail. Much of it was trans-shipped via the Camino Real to Chihuahua and Sonora, but Mesilla Valley merchants also bought wagon-borne merchandise from San Antonio. Wholesalers from San Antonio and St. Louis advertised in Mesilla newspapers.

Another boost to the Valley economy came from mining activity in the Organ Mountains. Legend has it that a dying Mexican soldier reported to a priest that a cache of gold lay buried in the Organs. The story has it that the padre found the gold but covered the entrance to hide the treasure, only to be killed before he could return to the site which has since been referred to as the Lost Padre mine. Similar stories have excited treasure hunters in the Organs ever since. As early as the mid-1850s discovery of a vein of silver drew many prospectors to Soledad Canyon. Many of the men who held leadership positions, politically or in the business community, were either mine owners, stockholders or personal prospectors, as Organ Mountain mining flourished in the last quarter of the nineteenth century.

Historic decisions, often made elsewhere in the country, were soon to impact significantly on Las Cruces. Although actual rail service was not to reach Las Cruces until 1881, railroad planners were well aware of the potential of extending their lines to the Pacific and its deep sea ports and gold. In 1853, scarcely a decade after the founding of Doña Ana, a railroad survey had recommended a southern and reasonably level route for extending rail service to southern California.

Following the 1848 Treaty of Guadalupe Hidalgo,

ending the Mexican War, Congress had approved the Compromise of 1850, which admitted California as a free state and New Mexico and Utah as territories without restriction as to slavery. The Compromise also set Texas boundaries as they are today and paid that state $10 million to forego its claims to New Mexico land. However, for the time being, land south of the Gila River and west of the Rio Grande, important to railroad plans, remained Mexican territory.

In accordance with the Treaty of Guadalupe Hidalgo, a joint boundary commission was appointed to survey the New Mexican-Mexican boundary. President Millard Fillmore appointed John Russell Bartlett as boundary commissioner. Bartlett's party of one hundred workers spent a half million dollars and discovered serious errors in maps used for the Hidalgo Treaty, but failed to complete the task. Col. W. H. Emory was then appointed Commissioner and completed the boundary drawing task.

Meanwhile, a man who was soon to become President of the Confederacy, Jefferson Davis, became involved. He gained knowledge of the border area as an officer serving in the Mexican War. Although severely wounded, he had heroically led U.S. troops to victory at the battle of Buena Vista. After election by Mississippians to the U. S. Senate, he was named Secretary of War by President Franklin Pierce. Davis convinced the President to send James Gadsden, a South Carolinian rail executive, as minister to Mexico. Gadsden's first assignment was to conclude border negotiations with Mexican President Santa Anna. The Mexican leader, desperate for funds, agreed to what is known as the Gadsden Purchase or Mesilla Treaty. The disputed 30,000 square mile strip was sold to the United States for $10 million and the deal was ratified by the

❧ Civil War ❧

U.S. Senate in April, 1854. A ceremony soon followed on the Mesilla Plaza, replacing the Mexican with the American flag. A painting depicting the ceremony hangs in the Gadsden Museum in Mesilla. Residents who had moved to the west side of the Rio Grande to retain Mexican citizenship had abruptly lost it.

The way thus was cleared for completion of the southwest link in a transcontinental rail line but the political and economic turmoil of the Civil War period delayed actual building for more than twenty years. Meanwhile, a federal subsidy enabled New Yorker John Butterfield to organize regularly scheduled stage coach and mail service from St. Louis to San Francisco. By 1858, the Butterfield Overland Mail was established and the first west-bound stage reached Mesilla. Two years later, Mesilla was designated the transfer point for a new Butterfield route to Santa Fe. As important as the Butterfield endeavor was to the desert southwest, travel was less than luxurious. Passengers heading west from Mesilla were advised to carry a rifle, pistol and/or Bowie knife and coaches had to ferry the Rio Grande behind swimming horses.

Slavery-related provisions of the Compromise of 1850 alerted New Mexico's newly appointed territorial officials that bitter confrontations over slavery lay ahead, either in legislative halls or on battlefields. The Compromise had mandated an election to accept or reject slavery once statehood had been achieved. However, as the nation moved inexorably closer to war, the New Mexico territorial legislature, unwilling to wait for statehood, passed a law protecting slave property already introduced into the territory. In its next session, however, the legislature repealed that act and thus appeared committed to loyalty to the Union cause. It all was a somewhat moot point, however, since census fig-

ures listed only twenty-two Negro slaves in the entire
territory.

Thus, initially, many New Mexicans, especially in the
north, remained indifferent and uncommitted to either
side of the slavery issue. The largely Mexican population
was aware that Mexico had outlawed slavery in 1829.
Moreover, Texas' decision to secede elicited little New
Mexican sympathy as Texan attempts to annex all or
part of New Mexico by arms or boundary claims had
been thwarted but not forgotten. It should be admitted,
however, that a system of peonage, involuntary servitude
and Indian slavery had existed in New Mexico for many
decades.

On the other hand, in southern regions of the territory, some secessionist sentiment was evidenced among
expatriates from Texas and other southern states. For
instance, in the mid-1850s, Doña Ana County probate
judge James Lucas introduced a bill in the territorial legislature to make his county a separate U. S. (slave) territory. Later he helped organize citizens' protest conventions at Mesilla in 1859 and Tucson in 1860, where plans
were made to organize a separate Confederate territory,
to be called either Primeria, Gadsonia or Arizona. They
established what they called the Arizona Provisional
Government, electing Lewis Owings provisional governor and Ignacio Orrentia lieutenant governor. By 1861,
they had organized two units of militia in Mesilla.

In early 1861, secession of southern states, formation
of the Confederate States of America and commencement of hostilities at Ft. Sumner, South Carolina, began
history's bloodiest, most destructive armed threat to the
unity of this country. The Civil War was to have both
short and long term consequences in New Mexico. One
almost immediate effect was that many of the ranking
U. S. army officers serving in New Mexico defected to

the Confederate armed forces.

Jefferson Davis, who had been actively involved in facilitating the Gadsden Purchase, resigned from the United States Senate, resumed his military rank of Major General, and was chosen President of the Confederacy. President Davis believed the Confederacy desperately needed a land corridor to the Pacific, which would provide access not only to west coast ports but also to California's gold fields He authorized Col. Henry Sibley to raise an army of Texans to begin that armed move to the west.

Texans ardently supported the pro-slavery cause and Colonel Sibley soon had enlisted a 3,000 man force. Lt. Col. John Robert Baylor soon headed west with a 258-man Texas Mounted Volunteer regiment, occupied El Paso and its Ft. Bliss, and by July, 1861, marched on into New Mexico. His forces occupied Mesilla without firing a shot and, in fact, were enthusiastically welcomed and provided with supplies by southern sympathizing Mesillans.

Union Army Maj. Isaac Lynde commanded a force of more than 500 well trained regular army men stationed at Fort Fillmore, a few miles south of Mesilla. When spies reported that Baylor's forces already were entrenched in Mesilla, Lynde ordered an attack on the village, which proved rather feeble and definitely unsuccessful. Lynde's men, despite being experienced veterans, suffered casualties and loss of cannons and equipment, and therefore hastily retreated to the Fort. The Major immediately ordered a further retreat to Ft. Stanton, one hundred fifty miles to the northeast. Ft. Fillmore's supplies and equipment which could not be transported were ordered destroyed.

Departure from Fort Fillmore was so hasty and ill-planned that the Union forces lacked food and supplies.

The most often repeated story of that Union defeat claimed that some, or even most of the troopers, had filled their canteens with whiskey rather than water. After a march of twenty miles east to San Agustin Pass, heat and whiskey had turned the march into a disorganized and even disoriented column of parched, famished, even fainting men. Historians disagree as to the accuracy and/or the significance of the whiskey story, but only one hundred men, at most, were capable of fighting. When Colonel Baylor saw the column of dust raised by Lynde's troops heading to the east, his 200 plus man mounted column soon caught up to the demoralized Union forces. He demanded and received Lynde's surrender, a surrender which turned most of southern New Mexico over to Confederate control.

History has branded Major Lynde a bungling coward, but in fairness, it should be added that his commanding officer, Col. Edward R.S. Canby (incidentally, a brother-in-law of Sibley) had instructed him to abandon Ft. Fillmore if it appeared it could not be held. Lynde also had false intelligence from Mesilla residents that Baylor had a force of at least seven hundred men and he knew he could expect no reinforcements of his own Union troops.

Colonel Baylor, a vindictive man, proclaimed that all of southern New Mexico south of the 34th parallel was now the Arizona Territory of the Confederate States of America. He named Mesilla its capitol, and named himself provisional military governor. While a number of Mesillans initially welcomed Baylor's forces, the Colonel's harsh measures soon alienated locals, especially after Baylor responded to local newspaper criticism of his tactics by fatally shooting the paper's editor, and then winning acquittal on a self defense plea.

General Sibley's three Confederate regiments had, by

❦ Civil War ❦

February, 1862, entered New Mexico and joined
Baylor's force, now re-supplied with captured Union
arms and supplies. After sending troops to occupy
Tucson, Sibley moved his troops up the Rio Grande
Valley. Union forces of Col. Edward Canby held Ft.
Craig, a few miles south of Socorro, constituting the only
obstacle to Confederate conquest of the entire Rio
Grande Valley and probably the entire New Mexico
Territory. Sibley's Confederates claimed a somewhat
dubious victory in the bloody battle of Valverde, success-
fully fording the Rio Grande but failing to drive Canby's
troops from Ft. Craig.

Confederate forces moved on north, capturing
Albuquerque and Santa Fe, and marched northeast
toward what they anticipated would be easy conquests of
Las Vegas and Fort Union. Confederate domination of
the entire territory would then be assured. However, at
the village of Glorieta, east of Santa Fe, Colorado reinforcements under Major (and Reverend) John
Chivington engaged the rebels, destroyed Sibley's supply
train, and sent the Confederates hastily retreating southward. A Santa Fe newspaper reported that of the more
than twenty-two hundred gray-clad troops who entered
New Mexico, scarcely a thousand survived to retreat to
El Paso and on to San Antonio. Sibley had lost nearly
twelve hundred men to desertion, disease, death and
imprisonment.

When Confederate forces seemed destined, prior to
the Glorieta disaster, to triumphantly implement the
Confederate strategy to win a corridor to the Pacific,
Union army officials in California began recruiting a volunteer force to defend their state. To their surprise, seventeen thousand Californians volunteered. More than
two thousand, including a number who were destined to
become post-war Mesilla Valley residents, were placed in

the First California Infantry Volunteers. Commanded by Colonel James H. Carleton, the First California was soon to be dubbed the "California Column." Most were raw recruits, originally from midwest and eastern states and several European countries, drawn west by the lure of gold.

By the end of basic training, alarming word was received that the Confederates not only had moved into New Mexico and occupied Mesilla, but had forced the surrender of Union forces from Ft. Fillmore and had even occupied Tucson. Carleton's forces were ordered into intensive combat training in the southern California desert near Yuma. When further word came that not only had Tucson been lost but that Gen. Sibley's main force had occupied Albuquerque and Santa Fe as well, the California Column immediately embarked on a forced march toward Tucson.

By June, 1862, the entire California force had arrived in Tucson, only to find the Confederates had retreated eastward eighteen days earlier to join Sibley's forces. Within a month, Carleton ordered another forced march, his destination the Rio Grande. Their first combat experience came at Apache Pass, near present day Bowie, Arizona, and the enemy was not Confederate but Apache. The Union troops, parched and exhausted, eagerly approached a spring at Apache Pass, only to come under withering Apache fire. A platoon led by Sgt. Albert Jennings Fountain stormed the Indian stronghold, caught them by surprise, and won the skirmish and access to precious water.

When the Column, 2300 strong, reached the Rio Grande, they learned the Confederates, defeated at Glorieta, had fled all the way back to Texas. Carleton was promoted to the rank of Brigadier General and was named commander of the Army's Department of New

Mexico, a position he held for four and a half years. Although there was little to suggest it, for months General Carleton was convinced that Confederate forces would soon re-invade New Mexico. He therefore kept his troops armed, drilled and prepared for that possibility. Their actual duty focussed, however, on enforcing martial law, checking citizen passes, confiscating property of Confederate sympathizers, and attempting to control Indian depredations. Fort Fillmore soon was abandoned, so many of the Californians were billeted in Mesilla or Las Cruces.

By 1863, Las Cruces had an estimated eight hundred residents. There also were 215 soldiers, quartered on Main Street and drilling in front of St. Genevieve's church. Las Crucens and Mesillans welcomed the Californians especially since government contracts brought considerable wealth to Mesilla Valley merchants. However, General Carleton's martial law certainly was less than universally popular. Merchants who had cooperated with the rebels had their property confiscated. For instance, Louis Geck had served as a county judge under the Confederates, so he was imprisoned for a time and his house and land were seized, but later returned. One provision of martial law involved confiscation of local farmers' excess grain supplies, ostensibly to prevent any returning Confederate forces from seizing them. In a related move, Carleton ordered closure of the two grist mills in the area, owned by Thomas Bull and Numa Granjean and then rubbed salt in the wounds by suggesting that in the future grain was to be ground by use of hand-held stone *manos* and *metates*.

Carleton also was criticized for his merciless approach to controlling Indian depredations. One of his orders to his troops was reported to be "You will make war upon the Mescaleros and upon all other Indians you may find in the Mescalero country.... All Indian men of that tribe are to be killed whenever and wherever they are found." He ordered Col. Christopher "Kit" Carson to re-open Ft. Stanton and to establish a reservation at nearby *Bosque Redondo* (Round Grove) to which all Indian captives were to be removed. Carleton's rationalization was that *Bosque Redondo* would provide its internees with opportunities to learn Christian principles and farming skills. Four hundred Apaches were the first to be moved to the reservation and they soon learned that poor quality seed, infertile soil and inadequate tools and supplies made the goal of self-sufficient farming impossible to achieve.

It was also under Carleton's tenure that a scorched earth campaign was launched against the Navajos, culminating in the 1863-64 forced three hundred mile "long march" of thousands from the Four Corners area to Bosque Redondo. The army soon learned to their regret that interning Navajos and Apaches together was "like putting a bunch of cats in a cage and then adding a pack of dogs." After years of increasingly disastrous circumstances including large numbers of fatalities from disease, malnutrition and inter-tribal violence, a more amenable site in the Sacramento Mountains was designated as a reservation for the Apaches and in 1868 the Navajos were marched back to their Four Corners homeland.

Carleton also established Fort Selden, fifteen miles north of Las Cruces, in 1865. Designed to protect *Camino Real* travelers the Fort was staffed for most of its service by black soldiers, often referred to as "buffalo soldiers." It was commanded in the mid-1880s by Capt. Arthur MacArthur, described by local newspapers as the most popular commander ever in charge at Selden. His young son, future World War II hero Douglas

MacArthur, recalled playing along the Rio Grande, leading to his frightened rush home when he came face to
face with one of the camels the army had experimentally
used as beasts of burden and then abandoned in the
desert.

It was in these war years that floods first put Mesilla
on an island and then left it on the east bank of the Rio
Grande. Because of martial law and floods, as many as a
thousand Hispanics took refuge in Mexico, at least temporarily, while others migrated to the Tularosa and La
Luz area. Political frenzy also was a factor in Mesilla's
decline in population and importance. In August of 1871,
the Mesilla Plaza was the site of a deadly riot, which
resulted in nine deaths and at least forty injuries.

The two candidates for New Mexico's non-voting
delegate to Congress, (territories could not elect voting
congressmen) J. Francisco Chavez and Jose M.
Gallegos, had come to town to address rallies of their
respective political parties. To avoid conflict, the parties
agreed in advance to hold their rallies in different parts
of Mesilla. Unfortunately, as the rallies broke up, and
the Fort Selden troops assigned to keep order had left,
the two groups, each led by its own band, came face to
face in front of the Reynolds and Griggs store on the
plaza resulting in a violent confrontation. One Apolonio
Barela allegedly fired a shot into the air. Democratic
leader I. N. Kelley then hit Republican leader John
Lemon in the head with a club, inflicting what proved to
be a fatal injury. Someone shot and killed Kelley and
mayhem ensued. An out-of-town district judge was
brought in to investigate the incident but left town quietly when he decided it was wise to let sleeping dogs (and
dead Mesillans) lie.

Most California Column volunteers had signed on for
three year hitches, so a number were mustered out in the

Fall of 1864. At that time they were paid $13 a month plus $5 a month for hazardous (Indian) duty. Those who mustered out at that time often had to walk back to California. The balance of the volunteers were discharged by 1866. More than 340 of them spent some part of their future life in New Mexico. A number became leaders in Doña Ana County and territorial affairs and as a group did much to provide stability and growth to the villages of the Mesilla Valley.

Among the California Column veterans who stayed in the Mesilla Valley were John Crouch, Lawrence LaPoint and the aforementioned Albert Fountain, all three of whom became politically active, were lawyers and ventured into newspaper publishing . Another was William L. Rynerson who owned several ranches, pursued mining claims, organized the Southwest Stock Growers Association, and had great success in legal and political pursuits. Others worked for cattle barons Oliver Loving, Charles Goodnight and John Chisum; cattlemen and merchants Morris Lesinsky and Benjamin Davies;

Main Street (city bakery and Second Class Saloon).

hotel manager John Davis; Capt. John Martin, operator
of a hotel and ferry in the Ft. Selden area; and community leaders such as John Barncastle and David Wood.
Another, Joseph Bennett, took the lead in actively pur-
suing mining interests in the Organ Mountains.

Rynerson, Davies, Fountain, Wood and Barncastle
all were active in formation of cattle growers and stock-
men's associations in the 1880s. However, the fact of
having shared Civil War experiences did not guarantee
that all veterans would get along amicably. Local papers
recounted tales of a street fight between Crouch and
Fountain. For his part, Rynerson became embroiled in
an extended political feud with retired California
Column Brigadier General (then Territorial Chief
Justice) John P. Slough. In a Santa Fe confrontation in
which Rynerson threatened to shoot Slough, the Justice
responded, "Shoot and be damned." So, Rynerson fatally
shot him, but whether damned or not, he was acquitted
on a self defense plea and thereafter led a successful and

1st Doña Ana County court house. (Site of Court Youth Center)

prosperous life.

An interesting contribution to the increasingly multi-cultural blend of the Valley population was the fact that of the eighty-nine California Column veterans who elected to stay in the Valley after discharge, seventy nine were married to or living with Hispanic women. Notable among these were Mariana Perez Fountain, Josefa Melendres Barncastle, Candelaria Lucero LaPoint and Guadalupe Ancheta Reynolds.

Chapter 4
▓ The Railroad and Stability ▓

The next major boost to the development of Las
Cruces was the arrival of telegraph and railroad service.
The army first undertook in 1875 to string telegraph
lines from Santa Fe and Albuquerque to Las Cruces and
Mesilla, to be connected with a line into Arizona and on
to San Diego. When construction funds were exhausted
and the line still had not reached the Mesilla Valley,
California Column veteran Albert Fountain led a fund-
raising campaign and another Column veteran, John
Martin, provided telegraph poles at $1.75 per pole.

Completion of the line to Mesilla and Las Cruces in
April, 1876, produced festive celebrations in both towns.
Gov. Samuel B. Axtell came from Santa Fe to lead the
Mesilla festivities. He employed the new electronic won-
der to send the message: "There is no more wild west. La

Mesilla is united with Washington, D. C. today."

In 1869 the Central Pacific and Union Pacific railroad builders had met at Promontory Point, Utah, and drove a golden spike to complete the nation's first transcontinental rail line. Expansion of rail service to much of the western United States soon followed. Scarcely two years later, the first train entered New Mexico from Colorado crossing Raton Pass. That line, the Atchison, Topeka and Santa Fe, continued to build southward, planning to link up with the Southern Pacific, which was building west in a delayed consummation of the Gadsden Purchase dream of a low-level route to California ports.

By 1880 there was such brisk, almost break-neck competition between railroad companies to push southwest and westward that they impatiently appealed to communities for contributions of land for rights of way and depots. The willingness of communities to offer such assistance could determine routing decisions. In fact, land availability was a major reason the Santa Fe bypassed Bernalillo and Santa Fe in favor of Albuquerque, arriving there in 1880.

When Santa Fe Railroad planners surveyed right of way possibilities through Mesilla, land owners resented their assumption that towns should assist them and were so slow to respond that the Santa Fe looked elsewhere. William Rynerson, one of the Valley's most astute business men, was well aware of the potential benefits to cities which encouraged railroad expansion to their communities. He knew that arrival of rail service to Albuquerque soon had tripled its population and that El Paso's population almost immediately doubled after the railroad's arrival.

Rynerson teamed with Henry Cuniffe and Simon Newcomb to quickly form the Las Cruces Town

❧ The Railroad and Stability ❧

Company. Jacinto Armijo already owned land west of the original townsite and he agreed to join the Town Company. They soon were able to offer right-of-way and depot land to the Santa Fe, an offer gratefully accepted.

In April, 1881, the first train arrived in Las Cruces to the joyful cheers of a huge crowd gathered at the west end of Depot Avenue (later re-named Las Cruces Avenue). Jacinto Armijo's son, Isidro, ten years old at the time, recalled that the arrival of the train was delayed until the crowd could be cleared from the tracks. He also remembered that the curious had to touch the engine, resulting in greasy fingers, and also had to inquire of the crew where they kept the mules to power the "iron horse." Later, many were delighted to accept a short ride, in reverse, offered by the crew. Territorial Chief Justice L. Bradford Prince glowingly predicted that the arrival of rail service meant the Mesilla Valley would become "the center of a very extensive and rich horticultural country ... large mercantile trade ... mineral discoveries of importance." The New Mexico Bureau of

Las Cruces in 1905 (note St. Genevieve's Church in background.)

Immigration hailed "grand opportunities represented in the mines, vines, valleys, mountains and mesas and its health giving properties, its majestic mountains and sublime scenery."

Although delayed by a flood at Rincon, the first passenger train arrived in Las Cruces in June, 1881. A few years later, a freight train bound from Albuquerque to Las Cruces was stopped at the Rio Grande bridge near Rincon by flood waters. The crew walked to Rincon and once the waters had receded, returned to resume the run, only to find no bridge and no train. The flood had washed away both. Fifty years later, a farmer's plow unearthed the edge of a buried box car. When contacted, the Santa Fe Railroad said the train was now the farmer's property.

Prosperous growth did develop in Las Cruces. A wooden depot soon was constructed and was replaced by a stucco and brick structure by 1909-10. Looking ahead, it should be noted that rail service continued for

North Main Street looking north.

over 100 years until passenger service was terminated in 1968 and local freight service ended in 1988. The old depot was bought by the city and designated an historic structure in 1992.

Las Cruces' population of 1,685 in 1880 increased to 2,340 in 1890 and nearly 3,000 by 1900. (See Appendix 3) New residents arrived from eastern states, Mexico, Europe and Civil War duty. These new residents started new businesses, became government officials, provided professional services, and offered support services for farmers of the Valley. Meanwhile, decreasing population and business activity had begun to affect Mesilla even before the railroad bypassed it. That village's population was 2,420 in 1860 but dropped to 1,578 in 1870 and to 1,249 by 1890. Partially because of the shifting Civil War political circumstances, the number of merchants in Mesilla dropped from twenty-five in 1860 to ten in 1870. In the same decade the number of merchants in Las Cruces increased from eight in 1860 to fourteen in 1870.

In 1887, the Rio Grande Land Agency, a sister company to William Rynerson's New Mexico Town Company, bought 5,000 acres south of their Alameda-Depot development and between Mesilla and the College. This addition became a popular residential area and came to be known as Mesilla Park. By 1888, Las Cruces had seven real estate firms.

One visible change saw a shift from building with adobe to bricks, mortar and wood. Another was growing concern over public roads. The territorial legislature assigned to the county probate judges the responsibility for road building and maintenance. In the 1850s, only unpaved horse and wagon trails existed and *alcaldes* were authorized to take down interfering fences. In 1882 the legislature passed a statute requiring every mature male to annually work on roads or pay an equivalent assessment. The most vexing problem in the Mesilla Valley was crossing the Rio Grande. Fords of the river depended on water level, ferries were far apart and the first bridges failed to withstand floods.

Automobiles appeared in El Paso in 1900 and in Las Cruces in 1904 and crowds were attracted to an exhibition auto race from Las Cruces to Alamogordo. New Mexico's territorial government called a "good roads" convention in 1904 and Doña Ana County held its own convention in 1908, an event which coincided with appearance of the first Model T Ford, owned by Brown Realty Company. The county appointed precinct road commissioners, and announced that fences had to go and bridges must be repaired.

Political consequences also soon ensued. When Doña Ana County first was formed, Mesilla was designated county seat. After a brief shift to Las Cruces in 1853, the county offices were returned to Mesilla in 1855. Despite intense Mesilla objections, newspaper feuding and even

H.H. Brooks, 1st Doña Ana County Agent, 1915.

litigation, the Doña Ana county seat, including court house, jail and various support facilities, which had been located in Mesilla for nearly three decades, had been permanently moved to Las Cruces

As a consequence of federal passage of the Homestead Law in 1862, all land in the territory except for Mexican and Spanish land grants was considered public land. A land office was established in Mesilla in 1875 and it also moved to Las Cruces in 1883. Land decisions were administered by a Register and a Receiver. The first Land Office Register was Lawrence LaPoint, succeeded by George Bowman. The first Receiver was William Rynerson. In 1876, the first Doña Ana County Commission was elected, chaired by Thomas Bull, succeeded by Jacinto Armijo, and then by Charles Lesinsky.

Among those who became prominent were Hugh Stevenson, Organ Mountain miner and his son, Horace, a many times county official. Martin Amador was a hotel owner and freighter and John Barncastle is remembered as a farmer, merchant and politician. George Bowman, was a banker from Pennsylvania; Lawrence LaPoint, a journalist and lawyer from Missouri; and Henry Lesinsky, a merchant from Prussia. Lesinsky and his cousin, Samuel Freudenthal, bought local grain and sold it to the Army.

Leaders of the Las Cruces community often had multiple interests and accomplishments. For instance, John Barncastle married into one of the Valley's pioneer families, wedding the daughter of Pablo Melendres, who was co-founder and first *alcalde* of Doña Ana and served on the Doña Ana County Commission and as County Treasurer. He became one of the county's biggest land owners. Eugene Van Patten worked as a Butterfield stage driver before the Civil War, was a Confederate army officer and commanded militia and home guard groups in campaigns against Indian predators and rustlers. He also served as county sheriff, built a resort at Dripping Springs, led construction of Loretto Academy and helped secure a land grant and build a chapel for Tortugas.

Martin Amador was a typical business leader. He worked at Fort Fillmore for six dollars per month and then was paymaster at the Bennett mine near Organ. He later took over his mother's general store, at Water and what now is Amador Avenue, which she had opened just a year after the founding of Las Cruces. He soon added a freighting business and added sleeping rooms for teamsters to his store. He also built a large home to the west of Water Street, which stood with the Amador Hotel as landmarks of the south end of the business district. The deteriorating house was razed in 1962.

One of the earliest mercantile endeavors, Henry Lesinsky and Company, was started in 1862 by Henry

Horse races were held on north Alameda Drive each Sunday.

❧ The Railroad and Stability ❧

Lesinsky and his uncle Julius Freudenthal. By the early 1880s, it was sold to Numa Reymond. Reymond, a native of Switzerland, not only operated a mercantile establishment on Main Street but also offered bank-like services. In 1884 he took Martin Lohman as a partner in general merchandise and livestock dealing. The Mescalero Apache Indian reservation had been established in 1873 and when Reymond and Lohman secured a supply contract between Las Cruces and Mescalero, they persuaded the Apaches to hire on as wagon drivers. The drivers occasionally brought their families and shopped at the Reymond-Lohman establishment. Reymond recalled they had in stock a surplus of tall black silk hats from the Lincoln era. They put them on display and tall black hats became quite popular on the reservation, especially among wagon drivers.

Phoebus Freudenthal and his father Louis opened a large general store opposite St. Genevieve's Church in 1882 but in 1888, a major fire destroyed the building and $28,000 in merchandise. Other merchants of the period included Aaron Schutz, who sold to Alfred Buchoz in 1883. Another notable mercantile firm was begun by Michael and Henry Cuniffe, who sold to William Dessauer and he then to Theodore Rouault.

Pennsylvanian John Lemon traveled to California by wagon train in 1848 and before settling in Mesilla in 1860 had run the resort hotel at Faywood, New Mexico, near the City of Rocks, north of Deming. He opened not only a mercantile store but a freighting business, serving Forts Selden, Craig and Cummings. He also opened a flour mill, powered by mules pulling two five hundred pound pumice stones. In the late 1860s he had served as Doña Ana County Probate Judge and later as customs collector but was one of those fatally injured in the Mesilla political riot of 1871.

As Las Cruces established itself as a major east-west and north-south crossroad and a railroad town, the hotel business began to prosper. Martin Amador converted his former teamster rest stop into "the finest hotel in Las Cruces." In the early 1880s, as the county seat moved from Mesilla to Las Cruces, Amador remodeled the adobe building to provide temporary space as a county courthouse, post office, jail and theater. The Amador Hotel building still stands and after serving several years as the site of Citizen's Bank now is the Doña Ana county manager's office complex. Louis Freudenthal opened a competing hostelry, the Don Bernardo, later named the Main, on Main just south of Court St. Drivers for the two competitors often raced their horse-drawn carriages down Depot (Las Cruces) Avenue to get first call on Santa Fe railroad passenger arrivals. Both hotels had restaurants and they even competed over which notables had been guests. The Amador was said to have hosted Teddy Roosevelt and the Don Bernardo had Woodrow

Dripping Springs Hotel, Organ Mountains, "Old Van Patten's"

❧ The Railroad and Stability ❧

Wilson and Pancho Villa, though not simultaneously, as guests.

Also popular around the turn of the century were the Rio Grande Hotel, offering a room, meal and corral space for two dollars a night, the Central and the Commercial Hotels, both on Main Street, and the Herndon and Campbell. Once Las Cruces' first County Court House had been built in 1883, on the site which became Court Junior High and, more recently, Court Youth Center, the Park Hotel was built to its west, facing Pioneer (City) Park.

While Las Cruces was expanding, at least in population, the physical size of Doña Ana County was shrinking. In 1863, Congress created Arizona as a separate territory. In 1868, Grant County was chopped off. Two years later, the northwest segment was added to Socorro County. In 1878, the eastern half of Doña Ana became Lincoln County. In 1884, land to the north went to Sierra County and, in 1899, the Colonel Fountain disappearance-related politicking moved much of Doña Ana's remaining eastern portion to create Otero County. In sum, in a period of thirty-six years, Doña Ana County was reduced from one of the nation's largest counties, stretching from Texas to the Colorado River and from Mexico to the Gila River, to an area of just over 3,840

Las Cruces Santa Fe Depot, 1901.

square miles.

The decade of the 1880s saw Las Cruces begin to stabilize and adopt the character which was to see it steadily grow and expand its services and potential to become the major city of southern New Mexico. Main Street still was a wide but treeless, dusty, sandy thoroughfare. One-story adobe stores and saloons and a few brick two-story buildings fronted by hitching posts lined the street. It was in this period that Main Street served as a political line of demarcation. Republicans frequented the side of the Palmilla Club Saloon and Numa Reymond's store, while the Democrats patronized businesses on the Albert Ellis barber shop side of the street.

However, there were signs of civic pride and progress. Between 1881 and 1883 sixteen street lamps were installed and in 1889 seventeen merchants contributed $160 each to insure regular sprinkling of the streets. One indication that the horse-and-buggy days were numbered was that complaints about a hitching post shortage went unheeded. In 1882 there even was talk of a street railway from Las Cruces to Mesilla, but the idea soon withered and died.

Interest in mining in the Organ Mountains waxed and waned, with the search for the legendary Lost Padre Mine always in the background . Silver and lead ores were discovered even before the founding of Las Cruces and what came to be known as the San Augustin Mining District produced nearly three million dollars worth of lead, copper, zinc and silver. By 1850, what was to be known as the Stephenson mine had been discovered and initially worked by Juan Garcia, original owner of the Brazito Land Grant. Hugh Stephenson was the first man to systematically develop his mines. A group of Ft. Fillmore soldiers bought his mine for $12,500 in 1858 and, as part of the deal, a crude adobe smelter was built near the Fort, but soon abandoned. During the Civil War, the Union Army claimed the mine operation but after the war allowed Stephenson to reclaim it. Basically, it was mining activity that led to the founding of the town of Organ in 1879.

As Commissioner of Immigration, Albert Fountain published a claim in the 1880s that mining had become the county's number one industry. Hotel operator Duncan McCowan even changed the name of his establishment from the Bon Ton Hotel to Miner's Exchange Hotel. Eventually, Joseph Bennett bought the Stephenson claims and renamed them the Stephenson-Bennett Consolidated Mine. In the last half of the 19th century that mine was said to have produced a million dollars worth of silver and lead.

Best known of the other mines was the Modoc, backed by William Rynerson, which had its own smelter. Others included the Hawkeye, Black Hawk, Torpedo, Memphis and Gold Camp, which for a time was owned

Modoc Mine, one of the largest Organ Mountain Operations, 1890's.

and frequented by Albert Fall, future U. S. Senator. Although most mining activity had ended by 1906, there were a few attempts to further develop abandoned mines in the 1920s and individual prospectors still roam the Organs. And, of course, descendants of "Doc" Noss periodically receive permission to search for the treasure he claimed was buried on Missile Range land at Victorio Peak. They now are involved in litigation with the Missile Range over what happened to the gold.

A number of short-lived weekly newspaper publishing ventures appeared in the pre-1900 period. Possibly the first was the Mesilla *Times,* published from 1860 to 1862. One of the reasons its tenure was so abbreviated must have been because, as mentioned earlier in this volume, its editor, Robert Kelley, editorially criticized Col. John Baylor during the Confederate occupation of Mesilla. Kelley was fatally shot by Baylor, who was never convicted of any crime but publication of the editor-less *Times* ceased. It was succeeded by such journals as Mesilla *Weekly Times* (1867); *The Borderer* (1871-75); and Ira Bond's *News* (1873).

Newspapers of the day tended to have strong political leanings, as when "Mr. Republican," Albert Fountain, and his California Column fellow veteran, John Crouch, founded the *Mesilla Valley Independent* (1877). Despite its name and repeated claim of political independence, it had decided Republican leanings. It also printed such denunciations of the Catholic Church and of marauding cattle thieves, that Fountain received repeated death threats and, in fact, his sons were subjected to ride-by shootings and arson attempts at the paper's office. It soon was succeeded as the Republican journalistic voice by the *Rio Grande Republican* , financed by William Dessauer, Simon Newcomb, William L. Rynerson and Aaron Schutz. For his part, once Albert B. Fall had established himself as "Mr. Democrat" of the Valley, he set out to challenge the *Republican* with his *Independent Democrat,* which he and/or family members published for several years. At approximately the same period S. H. (Harry) Newman began publication of what vacillated between being a weekly and a semi-weekly. It was called *Thirty Four,* so named because of a recent disputed election decided by thirty-four votes.

What probably was the most unique of all Valley settlements began in 1884. Dr. John Newbrough, a Cleveland dentist who had struck it rich during the gold rushes in California and Australia, arrived in Las Cruces with a friend, Andrew Howland. They claimed to have been led to Las Cruces by spiritual guides and then traveled north, blindfolded, along the Rio Grande. They were led to stop at a site a few miles north of Las Cruces and not far from Doña Ana and purchased twelve hundred acres for $4500. They thus founded the Shalam Colony, which they envisioned as a utopian community.

Amador Hotel Interior, 1921.

Dr. Newbrough claimed an angel directed him to a typewriter and for fifty weeks guided his hands as he typed *Oahspe*, which was a combination Faithist Bible and blueprint for founding the Shalam colony. Its mandate was to attract residents who would grow their own food, live righteous, dedicated lives, and assist with religious instruction of abandoned or neglected infants brought to the colony by Newbrough. Thirty five buildings, including a forty-two room dormitory, were built by the residents and laborers from Doña Ana.

As the children grew older and a trifle more rebellious and the residents tired of the spartan vegetarian and work regimen, complaints and, more serious, debts began to accumulate. When Dr. Newbrough died in the flu epidemic of 1891, Howland struggled for nearly another decade but finally accepted the inevitable, abandoned the experiment in 1900, and sold the land in 1907. Nearly a half million dollars had been spent in vain, seeking for utopia, and Howland did not appear to understand the failure. His explanation of the collapse was "... when you Valley folks had picnics at Shalam, you sneaked ham sandwiches to our children and once tasting meat, they couldn't help but sin."

The ladies of Las Cruces and the Valley may not have had a vote in the late 19th century, but there were activists among them. They founded what were believed to have been the second and third oldest women's organizations in New Mexico. A group interested in sharing literary interests first started meeting in 1884. By 1892, three of its members, Katherine (Mrs. Hiram) Hadley, Emma Dawson and Emma Davisson decided to start a club for "education and enlightenment of women." They soon were joined by Carrie Bowman, Carrie Lyon and Jettie Reymond. They first chose the name Arcadian

First Residence Building, Shalam Colony, 1889.

Club, but by 1896 were The Wednesday Club. In 1926, the name again changed to Wednesday Literary Club.

Their basic meeting activity was sharing of book reviews. However, in the earliest years, books were scarce and the only accessible retail book outlets were in El Paso. The only library was the small one at the college. They therefore depended upon a series of study group packets issued by the University of Chicago and called the *Bay View Course.* Over the years, the club's membership also produced successful authors such as Katherine Stoes, Ruth Day Johns, Stella Baker, Elnora Wiley, and Opal Lee Priestley.

Almost concurrently, another women's group, the Woman's Improvement Association (W. I. A.), was founded in 1894, with the primary purpose of improving life in the area. Mrs. Thomas (Alice Montgomery) Branigan, Mrs. John (Mary) McFie, Mrs. Numa (Katie) Reymond , Emilia Ascarate and Emma Dawson were the founders of what was considered one of the oldest federated clubs in the Southwest.

Their first "improvement" project was the result of seeing the casket bearing a deceased College faculty woman carried to the cemetery in an old wagon marked

"Coal and Wood." The club purchased, for $200, a black buggy with six upright plumes, embellished with gray satin lining, much fringe and many tassels. For a time, it was drawn by a black team for which Mrs. Phoebus Freudenthal raised money for the harnesses. The hearse was made available for a nominal fee of $10 in town and $15 outside town limits. The next project was to provide a sprinkler wagon. Homeowners could have the dusty streets in front of their homes sprinkled for twenty five cents and non-payers soon saw that the sprinkler was turned off at the edge of their property.

W. I. A. members had two other major concerns-parks and libraries. Funds from the hearse rental, street watering and ice cream socials helped finance development of Women's Improvement Park (now Pioneer Park) on what has in the past been called Station or Depot Street (Las Cruces Avenue). The park opened in 1898 and was termed "the first green spot in Las Cruces worthy of note." It now is starting its second hundred years of serving the area between the original town site and the depot. A few years later, construction also began on their W. I. A. Club House, which still stands today, and recently was bought by the city of Las Cruces for purposes of historic preservation.

In 1926, the first library, staffed by W. I. A. members, opened one afternoon a week in the home of Mrs. L. L. Roberts and then moved to the back of a millinery shop. By January, 1928, the organization opened their new club house just across Reymond Street from Pioneer Park and the library was moved there. Upon her death in 1932, Alice Montgomery Branigan willed $35,000 to help build a public library and $2800 to pay off the remaining mortgage on the W. I. A. club house. Branigan Memorial Library opened in 1935. By 1979, an extensive new library opened and the original Branigan

W.I.A. Club House on North Reymond.

began its metamorphosis to a community cultural center.

On another cultural front attorney, civic activist and Republican leader Albert Fountain moved his family from El Paso to Mesilla in 1873. Within a year he had organized the area's first amateur theatrical group, which became the Mesilla Dramatic Association. He often scripted, directed and played lead roles in what proved to be very popular productions. His sons assisted with staging and set construction and his wife and daughters handled costumes and makeup. After the relocation of the county seat to Las Cruces, the Fountain family followed in the mid-1880s and soon thereafter led in establishing the Las Cruces Dramatic and Musical Club. One of their most popular productions, presented at twelve hundred-seat Van Patten's Hall, was entitled *Pocahontas*. Scripted, as usual by Fountain, it was set not in Virginia, but on the Mescalero Reservation and even featured borrowed costumes and weapons from the Apaches.

Van Patten's Hall, located near the new court house, also served as a very popular roller rink and even a fair exhibit building. It was sixty feet wide, one hundred fifty feet deep and had eight windows to a side. In this period of cultural enlightenment, a community band was formed, subsidized by a public fund of $150. It played for roller skating parties and its Christmas concerts drew large crowds. In 1890 a Las Cruces Cornet Band was formed and in the 1890s, a St. Genevieve's Band also had been organized and played at much appreciated outdoor summer concerts. In 1887, a Southern New Mexico Fair Association was formed and the fairs featured commercial displays of local merchandise, farm produce, baseball tourneys, a grand ball and a Fort Bliss band.

Another measure of growth, if not of improvement, was the report in *Thirty Four* that in 1881 Las Cruces boasted eighteen saloons and five dance halls. A popular entertainment center was the Centennial Saloon and Billiard Hall across Main Street from the Rio Grande Hotel.

Some measure of medical care also came to the Valley. Dr. Oscar Woodworth formed and became president of the Southern New Mexico Medical Association plus operating his own drug store. By 1887 there were seven local physicians, including William R. Brewer, D. J. Johnston, James Booth, and J. D. Price, most of whom remained in the Valley only briefly. Small scale epidemics also struck the region in this decade, with an outbreak of pneumonia in the Tortugas area in 1880, malaria throughout the Valley in 1881, malaria and typhoid in 1884 and a scourge of scarlet fever in 1887.

It also was around the turn of the century that New Mexico, with its dry air and warm climate began to be considered an ideal site for tuberculosis therapy, about which more will be included in later chapters. The federal government announced plans to convert abandoned Forts Stanton and Bayard into the country's first federally funded tuberculosis centers. A sanatorium with open

Van Patten home, Dripping Springs, 1897.

air sleeping porches was built adjacent to Van Patten's
Dripping Springs Hotel in the 1890s. Dr. Robert E.
McBride, who was active in Las Cruces civic and medical affairs for many years, opened a tuberculosis sanatorium in 1904 on Townsend Terrace, just off Alameda on

Las Cruces Tennis Club, 1896. (Standing: Dr. Wooten, Dr. Jordon, Miss
Freeman, H.B. Holt, Sue Meade, Mr. Freeman, F.C. Barker. Seated: Edith
Dawson, Fannie Blakesley, Miss Granger, Millicent Barker. Seated on floor:
C.W. Ward, Katharine Stoes, Alice Branigan, Mr. Stevens, Jack Fountain.

Las Cruces' north side. He purchased a two story house at 1905 Alameda and added a row of tents. It came to be known to locals as the Alameda Ranch Resort, or just the Alameda. New Mexico has continued to be a haven for health seekers but new drug therapies soon sharply reduced the demand for sanatoriums.

By 1885, the *Rio Grande Republican* listed advertisements of five attorneys: the William Rynerson and Edward Wade firm and Simon Newcomb, Albert Fountain and Aikman Welch. Also advertising were jeweler Henry Piontkowsky, butcher James Ackenback, notary public A. L. Christy, pharmacist C. Butschofsky, and surveyors Sam R. Biggs and Lew M. Lampton. E. Chaves and Son also advertised their Organ Mountain Coach Line, offering round trip fares to Organ and back for $2 and offering to carry packages at the rate of 1/2 cent per pound.

Chapter 5
❧ Education ❧

Although New Mexico's Territorial Legislature did
not mandate territory-wide compulsory attendance at
public schools under a Superintendent of Public Schools
until 1891, concern over education of the young was evident soon after the Civil War. Earlier legislative sessions
had adopted a permissive approach in 1859, granting
communities the authority to operate schools from
November to April at a fee of fifty cents per month per
child. The Justice of the Peace was to hire teachers and
the Probate Judge was to supervise. Very minimal
progress was made toward a public school system in
Doña Ana County, however, because of shortages of
financing and of qualified teachers.

Even allowing for a possible tendency to exaggerate,
it is relevant to note that a Methodist missionary report-

ed that in 1870 he had found not a single public school in the Territory, labeling New Mexico "one of the darkest corners of Christendom." The 1880 census reported an illiteracy rate of more than sixty percent in Doña Ana County.

By 1874, the Mesilla *News* declared "We intend to fight until a school is located in every precinct in Doña Ana County." Similarly, the Mesilla Valley *Independent* ran a series of editorials calling for public school development and better trained teachers. One Albert Fountain editorial demanded that the legislature "give us a decent public school law, and don't forget to insert a clause prohibiting the employment as teachers of persons who sign their pay vouchers with an X mark."

In 1876 the county government had appointed a School Commission with Pablo Melendres, Jr. as president, but even then little solid progress was evident. Simon B. Newcomb and Thomas Casad started a public school in Mesilla, but in 1877, moved it to Las Cruces. Jessie Geck, daughter of pioneer Louis Geck, briefly operated a private school in the 1880s. An 1881 attempt at operating a public school again sputtered, with sixty-two students enrolled in January, but after financial constraints it closed in two months. It later reopened, closed, reopened, and closed.

History suggests, however, that late 19th century Valley residents were quite aware of the importance of, and were committed to, providing education to their children. Frustrated over the failure of legislators to pass a school law, there were even calls for the counties of Doña Ana, Lincoln, Grant and Sierra to secede from New Mexico. The proposal was to form a new territory, to be called Sierra, which would have schooling as its first priority. Such talk soon faded but when Simon H. Newman attempted and then gave up starting a school in

❧ Education ❧

Mesilla, he turned to journalism and his *Thirty Four* became an insistent voice and activist for educational reform.

Newman hosted a public meeting in 1880 at which attorney Simon Newcomb assumed leadership of a Las Cruces School Association. Contributors included Guadalupe Ascarate, Jacinto Armijo, Martin Amador, Henry Cuniffe, William Rynerson, Jacob Schaublin, Aaron Schutz, William Dessauer, Henry Lesinsky and Newcomb. They did succeed in raising donations of $1,000 and acquiring a two room adobe building at Amador and Alameda, which became known as the South Ward School. In 1882 the School Association sponsored a three night fund-raising summer festival and fair, held at the Commercial Hotel. Half-priced tickets were even sold in El Paso. The event raised over $1,000 and in December of that year, a five-day bazaar earned another thousand plus dollars.

Meanwhile, a number of church-sponsored mission schools attempted to fill the educational void. In 1881-82, the Methodists sponsored a school taught by Emma Hilton. A Spanish Protestant school operated briefly in the Presbyterian Church in 1885, charging from fifty cents to two dollars per student per month.

After Territorial Governor Lionel Sheldon warned the legislature in 1884, "The greatest want of New Mexico is a proper school system," that body again authorized local public schools and even taxes to support them. Martin Lohman was the first Doña Ana County School Superintendent, Lawrence LaPoint served as president of the first school board and Martin Amador was board secretary. However, Las Cruces schools still stumbled. The *Rio Grande Republican* reported in 1885 that the school board discharged teacher John A. May for not opening school on time. They hired Ida Jones as

replacement teacher but supporters of May started their
own subscription school, with the result that neither
school had enough students to function.

By 1886, Fred Lohman replaced his brother as
County Superintendent and in that same year, a committee was appointed to test teacher candidates. (Over a
century later, teacher testing still is controversial.) In
1886-87, Las Cruces Public Schools hired two teachers,
Katie Delaney for primary grades and John May, apparently forgiven for his tardy ways, for grammar grades.
However, fewer than 100 of the nearly 500 school age
children were enrolled. The school closed for several
months in 1887 because of bankruptcy, but when it
reopened, William H. H. Llewellyn paid for repainting
and refurbishing the school building. Another school closure came in 1888 as a result of a suit between Martin
Amador and Martin Lohman over ownership of the
building. Numa Reymond resolved that crisis by buying the building and selling it back to school directors for
$2,600.

Doña Ana County, outside of Las Cruces, may have
fared better educationally in these early years than did
the county's largest city. In 1888, for instance, records
show an estimate of twenty-eight hundred children of
school age in sixteen districts, with 513 of them enrolled.
However, for those students, the county was able to provide only fifty-five cents per pupil, which failed to cover
costs. By 1891, the county had thirty one precincts and,
therefore, as many school districts, thirty-one teachers
and over twelve hundred students. However, the only
Las Cruces public school operating by 1893 still was the
South Ward School on Alameda Avenue, originally
bought by the Las Cruces School Association. Its principal was C. W. Ward.

One reason for the tribulations of public education in

these early years was opposition, often well organized, by Catholic leaders. In fact, the Jesuit Order convinced some territorial legislators to sponsor a bill to grant members of the Order public school teacher privileges and, as partial compensation, to exempt Jesuit property from taxation. *Mesilla Valley Independent* editor Albert Fountain was married to a Catholic lady, Mariana Perez, and sent his children to parochial schools. However, his paper engaged in an intense and vitriolic editorial battle with the Jesuit Order and their newspaper, *Revista Catolica*. Fountain feared the Catholic proposal would severely thwart the early efforts to establish public education.

It also is significant to the history of the Valley to note that Albert Fountain was Speaker of the Territorial House in 1889 and shepherded a public school bill establishing educational standards and the office of superintendent of public instruction. It narrowly failed but another Las Crucen, Albert Bacon Fall, secured passage

Alameda Lane, 1897.

of a very similar proposal in the next (1891) legislative
session. However, it was not until 1912 that the legislature, by now a state legislature, authorized use of property tax money to pay for public education.

Possibly little affected by local newspaper feuding,
the legislature defeated the Jesuit-proposed and
Fountain-opposed bills and the arrival of Father Pedro
Lassaigne and Mother Superior Praxedes Carty in 1880
relieved simmering tensions. Both spoke out to calm the
animosity which had developed between private and
public school advocates. Presence of the two can be
attributed to the leadership needs of what probably were
the most important and stable institutions in Las Cruces
and the Mesilla Valley in the late 19th century, the
Loretto Academy and St. Genevieve's Catholic Church.

The Sisters of Loretto, pioneer educators, had come
from Santa Fe in 1870, because the sad state of organized education in southern New Mexico was so evident.
In 1852, the order had come from Kentucky to Santa Fe
and had established schools in Taos, Mora, Las Vegas,
Socorro, Bernalillo and Santa Fe. So, in the 1870s, five
sisters then made the ten-day, 290-mile trip, including
dangerous fordings of the Rio Grande, to Las Cruces in
two carriages. They first stayed at the home of Mrs.
William Tulley and opened a girls' school there. They
soon were able to purchase a fifteen acre tract of land
and an old adobe shack at the southern end of Main
Street. The school was officially known as the Academy
of the Visitation. Tuition and board cost $200 a year.
Day school students paid $5.00 a month for older girls
and $2.00 a month for intermediate and primary stu-
dents. Poor students were, however, admitted at no cost.

Mother Superior Praxedes arrived in 1880 and for
the next thirteen years the Academy prospered under
her leadership. She energetically set about improving the

Loretto Academy with buggy.

chapel and grounds of the Academy and convent, including the cemetery. Local newspapers referred to it as "a
physical and cultural oasis, the center of life for the
whole region." The Mother Superior was well aware that
financing in those days was as much a problem for private schools as for public and the first of a regular series
of fund raising bazaars was held in 1881. By 1890, a
large two-story Spanish style building had been erected,
with considerable assistance from Col. Eugene Van
Patten, and by 1897, a third story was added. Although
Catholic-built, administered and staffed, the Academy
was open to all students, both Protestant and Catholic,
and from time to time admitted male students as well.

As it grew and prospered, Loretto had forty rooms
and a library of 3,000 books. The Academy served the
community well until its final class graduated in May,
1943. The property then was sold to a group of
Franciscan priests in 1944. They in turn abandoned it in
1959, and by 1965 the Loretto Mall was erected on the
site.

The other major contribution of Mother Praxedes

was her active campaign to renovate or rebuild St. Genevieve's Church. St. Genevieve's was named for a young woman who saved Paris from Attila-led Huns in the fifth century A. D. It had been constructed in 1859 under the leadership of Father Manuel Chavez. By the time of Mother Praxedes' arrival, the church was deteriorating badly. Helped by parishioners like Colonel Van Patten, she convinced St. Genevieve's pastor, Father Pierre Lassaigne, to begin a rebuilding fund drive.

As soon as $3,000 had been contributed, construction began. Mother Praxedes' name headed the subscription list and whenever funds ran low, she organized another fair or bazaar. By late 1886, an imposing French style brick cathedral with landmark forty-four foot high twin spires rose, at a cost of $9,000, to replace the old adobe. By 1887, bells cast by Padre Doñato Rogiere were added, but were replaced in 1904 by new bells. Colonel Van Patten, during his term as sheriff, used prisoners to plant trees and grass. Father Lassaigne secured a fountain for the grounds and by 1888 fenced the property.

St. Genevieve's Catholic Church on north Main.

❧ Education ❧

Completion of the new church left one problem - a pile of debris from the demolished church still lay on and adjacent to the new entrance. When repeated requests for male assistance in removal of the rubbish produced no results, Mother Praxedes gathered the ladies of the congregation one Sunday and announced that on the next morning, the ladies would do the street clearing themselves. When the ladies arrived the next morning, the debris was gone. The men got the message. The church served Las Cruces from its central location on Main Street for eight decades until structural deterioration and impending urban renewal led to its demolition in 1967. Proceeds from the sale of the Main Street site helped construct the new St. Genevieve's which stands at 100 South Espina.

Although in its early years, St. Genevieve's was the city's only church facility, a number of Catholic institutions have since been constructed. They include Immaculate Heart of Mary Church (now a cathedral), four other churches, two schools and a Diocesan office building.

Another institution, Madonna School, originally was a home built in Mesilla Park in 1909 by New Mexico A. and M. president-to-be Winfred Garrison. When sold by Garrison, the structure was used for a time as the College's married student housing, but in 1928 was bought by a group of Sisters of Our Lady of the Good Shepherd from Cuernavaca, Mexico. The Sisters' mission was to provide a monastery for the Magdalens, a cloistered sect within the order, an orphanage for homeless and abandoned children, and boarding schools for Catholic children. Forty Magdalens and twenty Sisters built the dormitory with adobe bricks they made by hand.

The Sisters spoke very little English, could not drive

and had very limited funds, but survived in the early days in part because the house was adjacent to a field of carrots. Also, the Sisters were excellent embroiderers and by embroidery sales, doing laundry, selling bread from their bakery and with the help of neighbors and supporters, such as the Bissell and Stahmann families, were able to maintain the building. Mrs. Bissell would pick up laundry from homes in the area in the morning, leave it with the Sisters, then return the laundered items late in the day. Another boost from a patron was Adlai Feather's weekly late Saturday trip to local markets to pick up unsold perishable produce and deliver it to the Sisters. He also provided weekly bingo games.

The Sisters' primary mission was, however, to provide a home and school for unadoptable girls. The Sisters, volunteers, and the Magdalens handled the necessary teaching and maintenance chores. Eventually they housed and schooled about one hundred homeless girls. By 1960, the Sisters were able to open a high school for local young ladies, named Madonna School. All told, about 175 girls attended Madonna in its eight years of existence. However, by 1968, financial constraints forced the Sisters to close the facility. By 1969 they had moved to an Ysleta, Texas, convent and to sites in Mexico. The home/school building then was sold to builder Lewis Emerick. Mrs. Emerick maintains a chapel and small museum to preserve memorabilia from the forty year stay of the Sisters of the Good Shepherd.

For nearly three decades after the founding of the Mesilla Valley's first three communities, Mesilla's San Albino, Doña Ana's Nuestra Señora de la Candelaria and Las Cruces' St. Genevieve's were the only active congregations. Despite scattered local opposition, Protestant denominations began to organize congregations. They depended upon circuit riders and private homes, although in the 1880s, the Presbyterian church operated a mission school. Also, Thomas Casad and George Bowman each operated schools in their homes. The old courthouse and jail in Mesilla at one time housed a subscription school which depended for supplies upon Bibles and books or letters brought from student homes and used packing boxes for desks. A Methodist pastor, Rev. Thomas Harwood came to New Mexico in 1875 and when preaching in the plaza in Mesilla in 1891, became the target of oaths, hisses and thrown stones. He complained to his bishop that when a deputy sheriff passed and was asked to control the crowd, he refused. Reverend Harwood weighed one stone and found it was a two pounder.

Tradition has it that St. James Episcopal Church in Mesilla Park, founded in 1875, was the first Protestant church formally organized in Las Cruces and that St. Andrews Episcopal, on North Alameda, was founded as a mission church in 1911. Recent research has revealed, however, that a man named Barstow, a cleric and dentist, opened an Episcopal Grace Mission in Mesilla in 1871.

The gazebo in the City (Pioneer) Park.

He also operated a school in part of what now is the El
Patio Restaurant. He and one Henry Forester then
bought an adjoining building and briefly operated the
school there. Also, the St. Andrews sanctuary on
Alameda was not completed and formally dedicated until
1914.

Best known of the missionary preachers after the
turn of the century was Episcopalian Rev. Hunter
"Preacher" Lewis. Lewis came to Mesilla Park in 1905
and worked as a missionary for forty-three years.
When he arrived, the present St. James Church had
been built eight years prior (in 1897) by Joseph M.
McConnell and "Preacher" and his family considered it
their home church He was credited with establishing at
least seven churches and twenty-one mission churches
and serving as an informal chaplain to New Mexico A.
and M. College. One historian estimated that by 1914,
"Preacher" was "the shepherd of more than one-third of
the College's students." One source of his campus popularity was his willingness to play the piano for all sorts of
student affairs. He used whatever means of transportation was available, including bicycling and walking, as he
traveled up and down the Rio Grande Valley from La
Union to Belen. Legend has it that the first time he tried
driving a car, it crashed, and he never again attempted to
drive. In one year, 1930, he conducted 467 services at
sixteen missions. As he traveled, his favorite diversion
was knitting baby blankets and bonnets. He presented
knitted bonnets to each of the more than two thousand
infants he baptized.

The First Presbyterian Church was built at Las
Cruces and Alameda in 1883, and its successor was built
on Las Cruces Avenue in 1925. A Methodist Church
South was built on Griggs and was rebuilt in 1912.
Methodist Church North's congregation built at Organ

and Miranda but later sold that site to the First Baptists and built at the present site of St. Paul's Methodist Church at Griggs and Alameda. The present Methodist sanctuary has become an area landmark because of its "copper top." As mentioned earlier, the parishoners of San Albino Catholic Church in Mesilla met in a simple structure beginning in 1851, but in 1906 built its sanctuary on its present site.

One religious group tended to be a late-comer to the Valley. Although the congregation had been meeting earlier at Branigan Library, it was not until 1961 that the Jewish Temple Beth El synagogue was built on Parker Road. Ethel Perry, Alma Wagner and Jane Lieberman had earlier formed a committee of the Sisterhood to raise money and make arrangements for a Sunday School. It began in 1954 to meet weekly in the home of Lee and Frieda Trafton, with Nathan Wagner as one of its earliest teachers .

The latter years of the nineteenth century also saw the formation and popularity of veterans, business and service organizations. Col. Albert Fountain arranged a reunion of California Column veterans in 1874. This provided sufficient impetus for a more formal Mesilla reunion in 1878, featuring a memorial service, banquet and ball attended by two hundred veterans. Subsequent meetings around the territory led to establishment in 1889 of the Phil Sheridan Post #14 of the Grand Army of the Republic, with Fountain as its first post commander. In 1890, a G. A. R. auxiliary post was added.

The Masonic order came to New Mexico in 1846 with Gen. Kearny's Missouri troops in the form of traveling lodges. At the end of the Mexican War, members of course dispersed, but the Missouri Grand Lodge created four New Mexico lodges over the next twenty years. In 1866, work began on organization of a Las Cruces lodge.

Pioneer Park - gift to Las Cruces from Women's Improvement Assn.

By 1867 it was officially chartered as Aztec Lodge #108. However, by 1877, a Grand Lodge had been chartered in Santa Fe and the four New Mexico lodges exchanged Missouri for New Mexico charters, with the Las Cruces lodge chartered as Aztec Lodge #3. Aztec members such as William Rynerson, Simon Newcomb and Albert Fountain soon were active as Grand Lodge officers. Also, Lodge #15 of the International Order of Odd Fellows was chartered in 1891.

By 1900, Las Cruces had grown to a population of nearly three thousand and Doña Ana County had passed the ten thousand population mark. As mercantile enterprises proliferated in Las Cruces, a business and commercial club was formed. Named the C. S. L. club, it became quite active in community affairs and promotions around the turn of the century. Because members refused to reveal the meaning of the initials in its name, the *Rio Grande Republican* suggested facetiously they may have stood for "Cheat, Steal and Lie."

The next significant boost to Las Cruces' economy and future prospects also related to education, but at a higher level. As the pressure gradually built for New

☙ Education ☙

Mexico's hopes for statehood, territorial legislators knew
they soon should provide for the institutions which
would be considered appropriate for any territory with
statehood aspirations. In 1886 letters began to appear in
the *Rio Grande Republican* urging legislators to begin the
fight to locate a state higher education institution, prefer-
ably the agricultural (land grant) college, in southern
New Mexico, hopefully in Las Cruces. Letter writers
suggested one of the reasons for such a campaign was
"to keep our own boys and money at home."

A community's need and a man who could satisfy
that need met each other in Las Cruces in 1887. Hiram
Hadley, a member of the Society of Friends (Quakers),
arrived in the Valley just as "college fever" began to bub-
ble. He came remarkably qualified to spearhead development of higher education facilities in the college-starved
Southwest. He had written textbooks on language and
grammar and a book on Christ's life, had operated a
Chicago book store and had traveled as a publishers'
representative. He also had served as principal or head-
master of three different highly respected schools,

The old and new 1910 Mitchell Auto at what became Broadway Motel.

including Hadley's Normal Academy in Richmond, Indiana.

At the age of fifty-four, Hadley came to New Mexico to be near a son who had relocated in the Territory for health reasons. His first move, designed in part to prove his intention to become a permanent resident was to establish a realty company, H. Hadley and Company. He then bought sixty-three acres of valley land and his business offered loans at twelve percent interest. Hadley advertised that the Valley was "the most productive land on earth" and "investment will increase many fold within two years."

He quickly discovered that the only recognized and quality school in the area was the Loretto Academy, but he believed the reason the majority of school age children were unschooled was because of the Academy's "high tuition." In the words of Simon Kropp, New Mexico State University historian, Hadley "with great zeal ... set out to educate townsfolk on the need for schools."

By early 1888, Hadley felt enough public interest had been generated to call an informal "education" meeting in his real estate office. Once Judge John R. McFie called the meeting to order, Hadley was elected chair and attorney R. L. Young was to serve as secretary. Articles of incorporation were to be drawn up and sub-committees were appointed. Community leaders such as George Bowman, William Rynerson, Albert Fountain, Numa Reymond, Jacob Schaublin, Samuel Steel and Eugene Van Patten agreed to serve.

The group unanimously agreed to initiate a campaign to establish a college "equal in merit to any in the east." They listed the primary reasons for proceeding full speed ahead, which were:

1. Prospective rapid settlement of the Valley.

2. The large number of young of both sexes already in the area in need of quality education.
3. Imminent prospect of statehood for New Mexico.
4. The fact that no child could be sent away from New Mexico for less than $500 a year. With at least fifty children deprived of an education, it seemed practical to educate those children for $50 per year. That would mean $2500 would be spent at home, rather than $25,000 going out of the territory, plus the advantage of staying under home influence.

It was voted to sell $25 shares to raise an initial fund of $2500, but after four months, only thirty shares had been sold. Nevertheless, the corporation leased the two-room abandoned adobe at Alameda and Amador from Numa Reymond and announced the opening of Las Cruces College on Sept. 15, 1888. By mid-year, the faculty of three, including Hadley, were working with sixty-four students. Although calling itself a college, it might more realistically have been called a prep school, with students enrolled at three levels, elementary, college

Hiram Hadley in front of 1st college building (South Ward School) 1889.

preparation, and business.

Elementary students were taught at the South Ward School, while Professor Hadley worked with the older students in rented quarters at the DeMiers Building. Tuition was forty dollars per year for elementary students and fifty dollars per year for the college preparatory and commercial student, but fees were adjusted for those who could pass an examination. Hadley's salary was based on the school's income and near the end of the first school year, the treasurer reported income of $469.10 and expenses of $445.41, so Hadley's total salary for the year may have totalled $23.69.

A quarter century before, Congress had in 1862 authorized a land grant institution of higher education for each state and territory and in 1877 had authorized adjunct experimental stations to collaborate with each land grant school. It was anticipated that the 1889 session of the Territorial legislature would determine the location of the university, the land grant college, with its experiment station, the school of mines, prison and insane asylum.

Leaders of the Republican party and supporters of Las Cruces College urged Col. Albert Fountain to campaign for a seat in the legislature. It was agreed that once elected, he was to serve as spokesperson for Las Cruces' commitment to becoming the site of the territory's agricultural college and experiment station. Fountain narrowly defeated his Democratic opponent, newly arrived young lawyer, Albert Bacon Fall, and once in Santa Fe for the 1889 session, was elected Speaker of the House.

In his opening address of the session, Fountain committed himself to working for public education, equal educational opportunities for both sexes, (not yet a very popular stand) and equitable awarding of territorial institutions to various geographic sites. Citizens of Las

Cornerstone laying, McFie Hall (Old Main), 1890 - Cornerstone still stands on Horseshoe Lawn, NMSU

Cruces had actively lobbied for the agricultural college, financing the sending of delegations to Santa Fe and proffering tentative land donations. With adjournment approaching, Fountain's parliamentary skill pushed through the House an Omnibus Bill which awarded the university to Albuquerque, the school of mines to Socorro, the insane asylum to Las Vegas, the prison to Santa Fe and the agricultural college to Las Cruces. Gov. Edmund Ross quickly signed the bill and celebration soon followed in Las Cruces.

The *Republican* headlined: "Glad Tidings!! Las Cruces to Be Future Educational Center of New Mexico! All Hail to All Who Labored So Faithfully!!" A festive formal opening of the college was held before a standing room only crowd at Amador Hall. It was the first of the newly authorized institutions to formally open. The first Board of Regents consisted of Judge John McFie, president, and James Whitmore, Robert Black, Numa Reymond and William Rynerson, members.

The new regents quickly named Hadley the school's

first president, a position he held until 1894. They then moved promptly to award a contract for construction of the first permanent building, formally named McFie Hall but commonly referred to as Old Main. More than three thousand Las Crucens gathered on what has always been referred to as the Horseshoe for the September 9, 1890, ceremonial laying of the cornerstone for McFie Hall. Gov. L. Bradford Prince delivered the dedicatory address. The young son of Regent President John McFie attended under protest, saying it was "no fun standing on the floor and hearing papa roar." George E. King was named architect and the J. R. Bogardus contracting company won the construction contract. Remains of the cornerstone may still be viewed on the Horseshoe at NMSU.

President Hadley energetically prepared for the 1889-90 school year, including a trip to Washington, D. C., to secure a $10,000 appropriation for the college. With his own instruments he laid out fence lines and corners for the college farm. He started the college library with his own books plus a set of Encyclopedia

Old Main, 1st N.M College of A. & M. A. Building, 1891.

❀ Education ❀

Britannica which he had accepted from parents of a student in lieu of tuition. The first year budget designated less than $1,000 for library services, but the president quoted Emerson that "in the highest civilization, the book is still the highest delight," and by the end of the year had assembled six hundred volumes. He even found time, before the opening of the Fall semester, to host a Teachers Institute to which he invited Governor L. Bradford Prince.

During the 1890-91 academic year, the name of the institution was changed from Las Cruces College to New Mexico College of Agriculture and Mechanic Arts and the post office address changed from Las Cruces College to State College. It was another seventy years before the institution officially became a university, renaming itself New Mexico State University in 1960.

Although it was informal and unpublicized, Las Cruces' College of Agriculture and Albuquerque's fledgling university competed to be the first to award a higher education degree. Oscar Snow and Maude McFie were among the earliest students but a nephew of Judge McFie, one Samuel Steel, was on track to be a one-person graduating class of 1893, while Albuquerque's university would not have a graduating class for at least another year. Tragically, however, young Steel was shot to death as he delivered milk from the family farm. Las Crucens were so outraged by the crime that when a suspect, John Roper, was arrested, an immediate jury trial was demanded and conducted.

Disposition of the case happened to involve, by coincidence, the two rival Alberts, Fountain and Fall. Within two weeks, the prosecution, led by Albert Fountain, secured a conviction and Roper was sentenced to be hanged. However, on appeal, a new trial was ordered by the state appeals court, and its opinion was written by

Judge Albert Fall. The accused was then acquitted. Steel's murder remains one of Doña Ana County's unsolved crimes.

With no 1893 graduate, New Mexico A. & M.A. awarded its first degrees to the class of 1894. The five first graduates were Kate Agnes Williams, Oscar Charles Snow, Ralph Roy Larkin, Fabian Garcia, and Lemuel Charles McGrath. A graduate program was added by 1896 and the first master's degree awarded in the Territory was presented to Alfred Moss Holt in 1897.

A historical footnote should be added, thanks to former NMSU president Gerald Thomas. As an entomology student, Samuel Steel had identified for the first time an insect on creosote bushes. Entomology professors T. D. A. Cockerell and C. H. T. Townsend subsequently assigned the insect the scientific designation *bergrothia steelii* in honor of the slain student. Furthermore, in 1993, on the hundredth anniversary of Steel's death, the University's College of Agriculture established the Sam Steel Honor Society and in 1998, an honorary bachelor's degree was posthumously awarded to Sam Steel and accepted by his great nephews.

McFie Hall (Old Main) was the college's only permanent building for seven years, although an adobe engineering workshop was added in 1896 and the Science Building and a girls' dorm were erected in 1897. In 1900 the adobe engineering workshop was renovated to serve agriculture activities.

Fire proved a recurring hazard in early campus days. McFie Hall burned in 1910 and was replaced by the first Hadley Hall. By 1900 a group of shacks called Klondyke was serving as a sort of boys' dormitory. Students described Klondyke as "a synonym of physical discomfort and semi-starvation." The shacks were destroyed by fire in 1908, so by 1910 a boys' dormitory,

Hadley Hall, New Mexico State University, built in 1909.

a YWCA, Wilson Hall for agriculture, and a gym had been added.

The college's first quarter century was a period of struggle to survive. It was plagued by small enrollment, (it was 1907 before enrollment head count passed one hundred) a limited number of faculty and staff, meager funding and political shuffling of regents and top administrators. President Hadley was removed in 1894 and he moved on to the post of Vice President and Director of Educational Programs at the new University of New Mexico in Albuquerque. Between 1894 and 1901 three more men served as presidents of New Mexico College of Agriculture and Mechanic Arts, Samuel McCrea, Cornelius Jordan, and Frederic Sanders *(See Appendices #4 & 6)*.

The college's survival and permanence never was really in doubt, however. It had established itself as a permanent asset to Las Cruces and all of southern New Mexico. Its physical plant steadily developed and despite slow early growth and periodic management disputes, it was evident that its potential as a first class research university would ultimately be realized.

Y.M.C.A. Building, NMSU (west of present Recital Hall) and
the Gymnasium Building

After three years in Albuquerque, Hiram Hadley
returned to New Mexico A. & M. to teach history and
philosophy and later served on the college's Board of
Regents. He also was appointed to the Territorial Board
of Education, and to a term as Superintendent of
Education for New Mexico. In 1907, Hadley built what
has been referred to for ninety years as the Hadley
House at the corner of what now are El Paseo and
University Avenues. The two story home with broad
verandas often is inaccurately described as a former
presidential residence. A former college president,
Hadley, did have it built and resided therein, but not
during his tenure as president. The Hadleys resided in
the house until 1922. It was subsequently owned by
Russell and Julia Ludwick, and then by Don and Marie
Dwyer, who in the 1980s rented it to Lambda Chi Alpha
fraternity. Las Cruces jewelers Glenn and Sally Cutter
then purchased the property, renovated it to approxi-
mate its original appearance and floor plan and conserve
its historic beauty, and now operate their jewelry business at the site.

✿ Education ✿

For much of its history, the university has had buildings named for Hiram Hadley. For a period before it burned in 1910, Old Main was referred to as Hadley Hall. Its replacement as administrative headquarters and the second Hadley Hall was built in 1909 south of the present site of the Business College Complex. It was razed in 1959 and replaced by the present administrative office building, the third Hadley Hall, at the head of the Horseshoe.

Old science building, NMSU, built in 1897.

Chapter 6
☙ Law, Order & Statehood ☙

Residents of post-Civil War New Mexico had to accept that the distinction between law enforcers and law breakers often was very fuzzy. The governor who called southern New Mexico "a catch basin of rogues" no doubt was exaggerating, but a Lincoln County, New Mexico, sheriff was quoted as saying he had "Wanted " posters for 5,000 individuals, twice the number of people living in the county. A considerable number of Civil War veterans, especially veterans of the Confederate army seeking to escape new carpet bagger governments in their home states, headed southwest. Conflicts more often were settled by personal encounter than in the courts. Historians of the period refer to the code of the southwest as homespun law, which encouraged self defense and self redress. Law enforcement was sporadic and capricious, often non-existent. However, that code did stress loyalty to friends, family and employer, fair play, generosity, honesty, and respectful treatment of women. It also was generally accepted that you do not shoot an unarmed or unwarned man and you do not ambush an enemy or harm a woman or child.

Consequently, early day Las Crucens did not feel the need for sizable expenditures for law enforcement. Only when railroad construction crews arrived in 1881 was an official police force employed. James H. White served as police chief at a salary of seventy-five dollars per month. He in turn hired four patrolmen at a monthly salary of fifty-five dollars. After three months, when the rail crews moved on, the policemen joined the ranks of the unemployed. However, even after their departure an average of four or five shootings or stabbings per week were rather common occurrences and the police force was rehired. City residents also felt they could depend on elected constables to help provide protection. It was not until 1887 that the Territorial Legislature mandated that each county was to have a sheriff and two deputies and each town was to have a police chief and, apparently anticipating more murders, a coroner.

The three major law enforcement concerns of southern New Mexicans in the 1870s and 1880s were, however, raids and depredations by Apaches; cattle rustling, which had become so widespread that ranchers, large and small scale, were forming Cattle Growers Associations for mutual protection; and spillover from 1878's violent Lincoln County War to the east of Doña Ana County.

Once the Lincoln County violence had subsided, some of the survivors contributed to the other problems. During the War, Lincoln County Sheriff Matthew Brady had been accosted by a group of men and killed.

Although the sheriff was hit by sixteen bullets and it was obvious several men had fired at him, William "Billy the Kid" Bonney was charged with the crime. Brady's successor as sheriff, the legendary Pat Garrett, captured the Kid. Tried in Mesilla, the accused was defended by Albert Fountain, acting as a sort of 19th century public defender, but was convicted. Taken under heavy guard to Lincoln to be hanged, Bonney managed to escape, fatally shooting his jailers in the process. In 1881, Sheriff Garrett again tracked him down, surprised him in a late night encounter and killed him.

In those decades territorial governors often were urged to call out militia groups to augment local law enforcers and posses. In 1879, Gov. Lew Wallace activated the militia for a campaign against Apaches led by Victorio. Col. Albert Fountain led the militia in a series of largely futile pursuits of the Apaches through extremely difficult mountainous terrain. The Victorio-led band ultimately crossed the border into Mexico., where most were slain by Mexican *federales*.

In 1880, the legislature passed a new militia act authorizing communities to raise and equip their own independent home guards. Co. A, 1st Regiment, New Mexico Militia was formed at Las Cruces and Eugene Van Patten, William Rynerson and Albert Fountain were elected as officers. By 1883, a cavalry unit also was recruited. The 1st Regiment, New Mexico Cavalry, New Mexico Volunteer Militia, organized under Captain Van Patten and Colonel Fountain.

Another Lincoln County survivor, John Kinney, organized a gang for the express purpose of stealing cattle and transporting them, often by rail, to butcher shops in El Paso or Mexico. It was such common knowledge that Kinney made his gang headquarters in the Rincon area that it often was referred to as Kinneyville. In 1883, after numerous reported sightings and posse chases, militia captured Kinney and his wife near Lordsburg, more than a hundred miles west of Las Cruces.

Because Fountain had for some time led posses in pursuit of Kinney and his men, he considered the Kinney case a personal challenge. He led a patrol to the site and successfully dispersed a crowd whose intentions seemed divided between lynching and freeing Kinney. Fountain then escorted the prisoner back to Las Cruces and provided extra guards at the jail. He then prosecuted Kinney, won a conviction and personally escorted him to prison at Leavenworth, Kansas. Most Kinney lieutenants also were killed, or convicted and jailed. As a result, although the rustling problem continued, it was much less threatening to the ranching and Las Cruces area economy. Responsibility for anti-rustling enforcement was largely assumed by agents and attorneys for the cattle growers associations.

When Las Cruces won the county seat from Mesilla in 1882, Martin Amador initially provided space at his hostelry for a temporary court house and jail. In 1883, William Dessauer's bid of $23,874 won the contract to build a courthouse complex in the block bound by Gatuna (now Mountain), Armijo, Bonanza (now Court), and Barela, (now Reymond Avenue). Built on a 300 by 300 foot lot, it was a two-story brick with stone foundations, a metal hip roof, and a tower rising to seventy-five feet. It served for fifty-four years until the present court house was built between Amador and Lohman in 1937. That new building was financed by a $150,000 bond issue and $100,000 in WPA depression-fighting funds.

The most powerful attorneys in the 1880s were William Rynerson, Albert Fountain, Simon Newcomb and John McFie. Rynerson partnered with Edward C. Wade and Newcomb with McFie. District attorneys were Newcomb and Wade. The fact that the *Rio Grande Republican* began to report public hangings, with two in one week in 1891, suggested law enforcement forces had gained control of at least some of the criminal element.

The deadly political riot which shocked Mesilla in 1871 was evidence of how seriously Mesilla Valley residents took their frontier version of democratic process. By the 1880s, however, a review of the identity of office holders suggests electoral apathy may have set in, with familiar names and families appearing to control local offices. For instance, Pablo Melendres, Jr. served all or part of four terms as Probate Judge, one term as assessor and one term in the territorial legislature. Horace Stephenson was probate clerk in 1882, 1886 and 1888. Guadalupe Ascarate was sheriff in 1882, was succeeded by his father-in-law, Eugene Van Patten, in 1884 and his brother Santiago in 1886. Further evidence of apathy

Arcadian Club, 1895. Top: Mrs. F.W. Smith; Mrs. F.C. Burke; Mrs. S.B. Newcomb, Mrs. J.W. Dawson, Mrs. A.L. Christy, Mrs. N.L. Miles, Mrs. H.B. Holt. Middle: Mrs. Carrie Lyon, Mrs. A.E. Davidson, Mrs. E.E. May, Mrs. A.B. Fall, Mrs. W.E. Baker, Mrs. R.L. Young. Bottom: Mrs. P.H. Currie, Mrs. T. Branigan, Miss A. Miller, Mrs. S.A. Steele.

was found in the fact that only 356 Las Crucens regis-
tered to vote in 1884 and 363 in 1885.

While it oversimplifies, there was a tendency to
expect Anglos, especially those of Confederate background, to be Democratic and Hispanics to be
Republican. By 1888, however, two attorneys entered
the political arena and soon shattered the stereotypes
and the apathy. Both had studied law in the offices of
distinguished jurists but came from very different backgrounds and had equally different political philosophies.

Albert Fountain, born in 1838 to a well-to-do New
York family, had considerable formal education before
turning an educational tour of Europe into an around-
the-world series of misadventures which terminated in
California. After working at various gold-field related
jobs, then as a newspaper correspondent reporting on
Central American revolutions, he began to study law.
Just as he completed preparations for the California bar
exam, Union army recruiters began to seek volunteers to
serve in the California Column, which was to repulse
any Confederate thrust toward the Pacific coast.

Fountain thrived on army life, arrived in the Mesilla
Valley with the California Column, earned regular promotions, and soon was serving in Indian control and
martial law enforcement campaigns in the Mesilla Valley.
He married a young Mesillan, Mariana Perez, and
expected to settle in that village. However, when he was
seriously injured in a campaign to chase Navajo escapees
back to *Bosque Redondo,* he was transported to El Paso to
recuperate and opted to settle in that Texas city.

With a natural affinity for political activity, he soon
was elected to the Texas Senate and led that state's fight
to recant its secessionist past and win re-admission to the
Union. Fountain soon learned there was no problem of
apathy in post-Civil War Texas politics. When he

Col;. Albert Jennings Fountain

attempted to protect Mexican and Indian access to salt beds east of El Paso, he was met with bribery offers and death threats. He later was shot in a confrontation with a frustrated political appointment seeker and, after his attacker had fatally shot a local judge, Fountain led an impromptu posse which killed the job seeker. From that point on, political opponents unfairly but effectively painted Fountain as a murderer. Therefore, the El Paso political climate made an 1873 move to New Mexico and what he called "the placid village of Mesilla" seem advisable. It must be assumed that Fountain either did not know about or forgot or chose to ignore the riot which had disrupted Mesilla's quiet placidity scarcely two years before.

Fountain quickly established a successful law practice, proved himself a political activist and ventured into and out of newspaper publishing. His primary political goal, which was to energize the local Republican party faithful, was so successfully accomplished that he soon was referred to as "Mr. Republican". He vigorously led

⚘ Law, Order & Statehood ⚘

Mesilla's fight to retain its status as Doña Ana County seat, but when it became obvious that Las Cruces was to replace Mesilla as the seat of county government and judicial proceedings, the Fountains moved to the larger city.

By 1888, after fifteen years of leading GOP organizing and election campaigns, Fountain was asked to run for a seat in the territorial lower house and in so doing to manage Las Cruces' quest to win location of the future state's agricultural college in the Mesilla Valley. His election appeared assured. Meanwhile, however, a young Kentuckian named Fall had located in Las Cruces, not yet realizing he was destined to challenge the Fountain political career.

Albert Bacon Fall was born in 1861, the son and nephew of Confederate army officers. He had ignored family urgings that he enter the Protestant ministry and had instead successfully taught school. Respiratory illness led him west, however, where he worked as a cowhand, trail boss and camp cook on cattle drives, then in retail trade, and also as a hard rock miner in Mexico and, ultimately in New Mexico. His experience in Mexico enabled him to develop reading and speaking fluency in Spanish and established personal and business relationships with the Mexican people.

As he worked as a miner in the Kingston area, Fall received word that the young lady he had married during his Texas wanderings, Emma Morgan, had become ill. In 1887, Fall moved her and their children to Las Cruces, staying initially at the Commercial Hotel. The family soon moved to a house which still stands at 311 South Miranda Street. He initially opened a stationery store and helped organize the Building and Loan Association, but with a natural assertiveness and a southern Democrat heritage he was almost immediately

Senator Albert Bacon Fall

involved in reviving the local Democratic party.

Once admitted to the New Mexico bar, he agreed to oppose Albert Fountain in the 1888 race for the Territorial House seat. It became a contest between the long time resident Republican and the youthful newcomer Democrat. The local Republican press characterized Fall as a "pygmy and a baby" beside the experienced Fountain. To the surprise of many long time Las Crucens, Fall turned the "sure thing" Fountain victory into a closely contested race. Fountain was victorious, however, and once in Santa Fe was elected Speaker of the House. It was in this role that he successfully carried the legislation which brought the agricultural college to Las Cruces.

Fall vowed never to run for political office again, but soon was back to building a Democratic base, especially among the Hispanic voters. He even campaigned in La Mesilla as "Alberto" B. Fall and before long began to be referred to as "Mr. Democrat." His success is evidenced by the fact that the 1888 legislative race was the only contested election he ever lost. The two opposed each other for the legislative seat again in 1890, with Fall the

victor. Results of this election and those of 1892 and
1894 were protested and recounts demanded but in each
case the victories of Fall and his candidates were sustained.

An 1892 election day confrontation illustrated the
Las Cruces political climate of the 1890s. Fall was the
Democratic candidate for a seat in the legislative upper
house (or Council) and was a strong favorite. In desper-
ation, Republican leaders predicted Democrat-inspired
voter fraud and announced they were calling out the
militia to supervise the election. Fall labeled this a bla-
tant attempt to intimidate voters, so he sent word to his
old friend and supporter, rancher Oliver Lee.
Accompanied by his cowhands, Lee rode all night from
his ranch south of Alamogordo. At dawn, the adobe
parapet of the Martin Lohman general store, directly
across Main Street from the polling site, was lined with
Lee riflemen fully supplied with weapons and ammunition from the Lohman store.

When Maj. W. H. H. Llewellyn and Capt. Thomas
Branigan marched the militia company up Main Street
to assume guard positions at the polls, another politics-
related Mesilla Valley riot seemed imminent. At the critical moment Albert Fall stepped into the street, raised his
arms, explained that he simply wanted to insure that his
supporters were not intimidated, then shouted,
"Llewellyn, get the hell out of here with that damned
militia within two minutes or I will have you all killed."
Major Llewellyn conferred with Captain Branigan for
considerably less than two minutes, and the militia
marched back down the street. Fall later explained that
he had received information that an assassination plot
was aimed at him. He did win the election but probably
would have done so without the show of force.

Albert Fall went on to a highly successful law practice and business career. He claimed to have represented defendants in 500 rustling cases without a single conviction and that of the many murder suspects he defended, only one was convicted. He served as territorial attorney general, Associate Judge of New Mexico's Third Judicial District, and additional terms in the Territorial Upper House. He was an elected delegate to conventions called to draft a constitution, prerequisite to winning statehood for New Mexico. Once statehood was achieved, Fall, by now a Republican, was one of New Mexico's first two United States Senators. After nine years in the Senate, during which he came to be considered that body's expert on Mexican affairs, he ultimately served as Secretary of the Interior in President Harding's cabinet, the first resident New Mexican to be appointed to a cabinet level position.

For his part, Albert Fountain continued to work actively for GOP causes but devoted his energies in the 1890s primarily to serving as investigator and prosecutor of cattle rustler defendants, representing cattle grower associations. But that just meant Fall-Fountain animosities intensified. This was because Fall had long standing friendly and professional relationships with the small scale ranchers, largely of Texan background. These men lived by the tradition that, especially during cattle roundup time, finders of "stray" calves were keepers, not thieves or rustlers.

As Fountain actively sought rustling indictments, an armed confrontation occurred in 1895, again on Las Cruces' Main Street. Fountain and Constable Ben Williams came face to face with Albert Fall and his brother-in-law, Joe Morgan. A number of shots were fired but neither the eye witnesses nor the two local newspapers, mouth pieces for the two political parties, could agree on who fired first. Both Morgan and

Williams were slightly injured. When called into session, the grand jury, made up of sixteen Democrats and five Republicans, refused to indict either Fall or Morgan, but instead indicted Williams and Fountain. The judge would not accept this, so both Fountain and Williams were then indicted on unrelated charges which soon were dropped. Fall's newspaper explained that he "had simply succumbed to a personal dislike of Williams and decided to take a shot at him; for wasn't that any free-born New Mexican's right and privilege?"

Four months later, in January, 1896, Fountain felt he had sufficient evidence to seek thirty-two rustling and brand-defacement indictments against twenty-three small scale ranchers, including friends of Fall. A special term of the court was scheduled in Lincoln and was to consist of both a grand jury session and District civil and criminal proceedings. Fountain had received death threats and knew of one botched conspiracy to assassinate him. His family wanted his oldest son to travel with him but circumstances prevented it, so eight-year old son Henry accompanied the Colonel. The family probably thought the presence of an eight year old would make any attempt on the Colonel's life most unlikely.

Father and son completed the hundred-twenty mile trip without serious incident and the jury handed down the indictments Fountain sought. Although he was subjected to angry verbal outbursts in the courtroom and was handed a death threat note as he departed the court house, the Fountains declined offers to provide escorts or to accompany them. So, father and son started the three day trip home, scheduled to arrive on Sunday, Feb. 1, 1896.

That Sunday afternoon, they met and conversed with a mail carrier, to whom the Fountains confided that they had noticed riders following them, silhouetted against the sky but too distant to be identified. When the mail man urged them to accompany him back to a nearby mail station and travel on to Las Cruces together the next day, the Colonel explained he had court business in Silver City the following day and that little Henry was suffering from a cold and needed his mother's care. Within hours after that conversation, they disappeared and were never seen or heard from again. As soon as it became evident they were not going to arrive on schedule at the Fountain home, an informal posse set out immediately, followed by search parties. They found evidence in a desert area known as Chalk Hill, scarcely thirty miles from home, which suggested the Fountains had been ambushed and apparently killed.

Sizable rewards were offered and the territorial governor hired Pinkerton agents to investigate, but to no avail. The few potential leads produced no solid evidence and more important, there were no *corpi delicti*, no bodies ever were found. Under pressure from New Mexico's

Henry J. Fountain, age 8.

Gov. W. T. Thornton and county officials, Numa
Reymond, the duly elected sheriff, agreed to take an
extended vacation, permitting the county to hire Billy
the Kid-killer Patrick Floyd Garrett to solve the case.
Garrett was heavily in debt and welcomed the proffered
$300 per month pay. Yet, even though he had his eye on
that $10,000 reward, it took Sheriff Garrett two years to
file charges.

Not even the reward inducement produced solid evidence over the next two years, but Garrett and the
town's leading Republican citizens believed from day one
that Oliver Lee and his hired hands, Jim Gilliland and
Bill McNew, committed the crime at the behest of Fall.
In fact, that explained why posses and searchers from
the day after the disappearance headed toward Oliver
Lee's ranches. On the other hand, Albert Fall, Oliver
Lee and his Democratic small-scale cattle growing
friends ridiculed the idea of their involvement.

As legal maneuvering dragged on, Lee and Gilliland
went into hiding at the isolated ranch of cowboy-author
Eugene Manlove Rhodes, claiming they would not survive in the custody of Pat Garrett. Bill McNew finally
was arrested, however, and spent many months in jail.
After Lee and Gilliland finally turned themselves in,
prosecution attorneys opted to try them first for the murder of young Henry, hoping to play on the emotions of
the jury. Of course, Albert Fall defended them. He first
managed to move the trial from Doña Ana County by
brokering the creation of a new county, Otero, and
drawing its western boundary line so that the alleged
murder occurred in that county. Because the new county
had only the most limited judicial facilities in place, Fall
then secured a change of venue to Sierra County and its
county seat, the village of Hillsboro.

The trial began in late May, 1899, well over three

years after the disappearance. It lasted eighteen days, was conducted before a very partisan, pro-Fall crowd and attracted what was, for the late 19th century, extraordinary media attention. At times it assumed characteristics of a cross between a political debate and a legal circus. Prosecution and defense each employed three well known attorneys. The prosecution was led by Republican and Santa Fe Ring kingpin Thomas Catron and, of course, Mr. Democrat, Albert Fall, led the defense. Nearly fifteen years later the two were to become New Mexico's first two U. S. Senators.

Both because of the failure to find bodies and because Fall not only handled prosecution witnesses masterfully but delivered a fiery final summary, the jury needed only eight minutes to return an acquittal verdict. Other charges ultimately were dropped, so no one ever was tried for the murder of the Colonel. A memorial stone marking reserved burial spaces for Albert Fountain and his son stands in Las Cruces' Masonic Cemetery. At least two unproductive searches for the Fountain remains have combed the San Andreas

Chalk Hill, site of dissappearance of Albert & Henry Fountain.

Mountains over the years and, in fact, two such searches were conducted near the Sacramento River, south of Timberon, as recently as late 1997.

The acquittal left Sheriff Pat Garrett without the reward money he had coveted. He was re-elected in 1898, but as that term ended he found himself deeply in debt, gambling and borrowing heavily and dodging creditors. When a new gym was dedicated in Las Cruces, he let himself be talked into a boxing match with an opponent known as Dr. Roger. The fight was declared a draw but did provide Garrett with enough dollars to temporarily placate his most persistent creditors. He then moved to Texas, but in 1905 settled into a ranch near San Agustin Pass.

Garrett soon discovered that not even horse breeding was profitable enough to support a family of eight children. It was whispered around town that the real reason Garrett settled almost within sight of the Fountains' disappearance site was that he still hoped he might find the Fountain remains and/or their ambushers and win that still available reward. A neighboring rancher, W. W. Cox held a mortgage on the Garrett property. When an opportunity developed to sell the ranch, Garrett and potential buyers headed toward Las Cruces to close the deal. Midway between Organ and Las Cruces, Garrett was fatally shot. Wayne Brazel, an employee of Cox, immediately confessed to the killing, was defended by Albert Fall and was acquitted on a plea of self defense. Some historians, citing ballistic evidence, have expressed serious doubt that Brazel was the murderer and certainly doubt that whoever fired the fatal shots did so in self-defense.

The best known member of Garrett's surviving family was daughter Elizabeth. Although blind, she was a talented musician and composed what became New

Sheet music cover page, Elizabeth Garrett's "Oh Fair New Mexico," 1917.

Mexico's state song, *"O Fair New Mexico.* " A memorable event in pre-World War I Las Cruces occurred in 1915 when Elizabeth and her guide dog Tenne visited Central School and she played and sang her *"O Fair New Mexico"* for the students.

In 1898, during the period of Pat Garrett's on-going investigation and search for suspects, Albert Fall was otherwise occupied. Early in that year, the U. S. battleship Maine was mysteriously blown up in the harbor of Havana, Cuba, with the loss of 260 American crew men. The U. S. blamed Spain and on April 24, 1898, declared war on Spain. Teddy Roosevelt resigned as Assistant Secretary of the Navy and he and friend Leonard Wood, a surgeon and Army officer, announced plans to recruit a body of men who could "ride horses and shoot" to go win the war in Cuba. In those days it seemed a very macho adventure and 23,000 men volunteered, although only about 1,000 were chosen. The New Mexico volunteers, totalling 358, were commanded by future territorial governor George Curry. Fourteen were from the Las

Cruces area including Fall, Capt. William H. H. Llewellyn, his son Morgan Llewellyn, Ralph McFie, Numa Frenger, and Edwin E. Casey.

Albert Fall, intensely patriotic, notified New Mexico Gov. Miguel Otero that he personally would recruit, from Las Cruces, fifty sharp-shooters to fight independently under his command. When the governor expressed considerable doubt about the "independent command" request, Fall sought to win command of the local militia company then led by an obviously aging Eugene Van Patten.

When Governor Otero came to Las Cruces to swear Van Patten's company into the regular army, Fall begged to be made captain of the local company. Fall's friends supported him and to the governor's surprise, so did local Republican leaders. When the GOP leaders explained, however, that this would be on condition that Fall never could return to Doña Ana County after the war, the governor understood the apparent inconsistency. He laughingly assured them he would never accede to such a condition. He had, however, already talked Van Patten into resigning his captaincy in exchange for a lieutenant colonel's commission in the national guard. He then appointed Fall as Captain of Company H. The governor reported Fall jumped for joy and ran all the way to the company camp. Captain Fall served for several months and was accorded high marks by his superiors. He was transferred to a camp in Georgia and hoped to be on his way to Cuba, but the end of the war intervened.

The main body of southwestern volunteers trained in San Antonio, Texas, and 850 of them then entrained for Tampa, Florida. Some called them Teddy's Terrors, the Texas Tarantulas, or the Cowboy Contingent but in time the nickname Roosevelt's Rough Riders stuck. They landed in Cuba in June,1898, and Roosevelt led them in charges up San Juan and Kettle Hills. One in three of the Rough Riders would be killed, wounded or disabled by yellow fever or malaria. One former New Mexico College of Agriculture student, Edwin E. Casey, died from yellow fever while serving as a member of Co. H, the only Aggie to die in Spanish-American War service. Because of his gratitude for the patriotism and fighting skill of volunteers from Arizona and New Mexico, Teddy Roosevelt vowed to actively push for statehood for the two territories.

Throughout this period, New Mexico (and Arizona, which had been created by Congress as a separate territory in 1863) had languished in step-child like territorial status, repeatedly sending delegates and overtures to Congress regarding statehood. Despite evidence of federal legislators harboring deplorable religious and ethnic prejudices, Congress had come near to passing a statehood bill in 1874. Opponents kept repeating exaggerated claims that of 158 churches in the New Mexico territory, 152 were Catholic and that the territory's six Protestant churches could seat 850 people, while the Catholic sanctuaries could seat 80,000. They also claimed that of 60,000 New Mexico inhabitants aged ten years or older, 48,000 could not read and more than 52,000 could not write.

New Mexico's Congressional delegate, Stephen B. Elkins, succeeded in refuting such charges but just before the 1874 vote, a little known congressman from Michigan, Julius Caesar Burrows, did him in. Burrows delivered a fiery floor speech castigating the South, its culture and the Ku Klux Klan. Elkins entered the House chambers just as the Michigander concluded his speech via an entrance which placed him nearest to Burrows. Hearing applause as he entered but having no knowledge of the nature of the speech, he enthusiastically shook Burrows' hand in clear view of the angry southern congressmen whose votes he desperately needed for the statehood bill. New Mexico failed to win statehood by a scant seven votes and for the next three decades or more, New Mexicans lamented that "fateful handshake."

Finally winning statehood in 1912 was the event which next boosted the Mesilla Valley and Las Cruces. A prerequisite to the awarding of statehood was adoption of a state constitution acceptable to Congress and territorial voters. Albert Fountain's final elected civic service was as a delegate to a Constitutional Convention held in 1889. The document developed by the fifty-three delegates received considerable public and media support but Democratic leaders, including Albert Fall, launched an ethnic and Catholic oriented counter-attack claiming Hispanic children would be forced to attend public schools and their parents would be heavily taxed to pay for those schools. The proposed constitution was rejected by the electorate by more than a two-to-one margin.

In 1898, statehood impatience spawned an incident which stirred much discussion but little action. One Harry Block announced plans to petition for a new state, to be comprised of Socorro, Sierra, Doña Ana, Otero, Lincoln, Chavez and Eddy counties in New Mexico, Cochise, Graham and part of Apache counties in Arizona and that part of Texas south of New Mexico. He explained that such a move would address a common problem of the three areas, in that southern New Mexico was ignored by its Territorial legislature in Santa Fe, just as West Texas was ignored by Austin and eastern Arizona felt neglected by Phoenix. The new state was to be named Sacramento, with El Paso the capitol city.

The proposed merging of the interests of counties from three states soon disintegrated. Veteran New

Mexico legislator W. H. H. Llewellyn introduced a memorial in his territory's legislature calling for a meeting of lawmakers and citizens on July 4, 1899, to discuss including all of New Mexico in the proposed new territory. Not wanting to wait until July 4 or let New Mexicans seize the initiative, a group of El Paso businessmen called a "new state" convention for noon, March 16, 1899. New Mexico delegates attended their own caucus that morning and agreed to boycott the noon meeting. Judge Joseph Crosby chaired the noon affair, which quickly adopted a motion that the new state idea was "impractical, inexpedient and undesirable and should be allowed to rest in peace," and it was.

By the turn of the century, statehood advocates began to hear promises of aid in high places. As men-

Ex-president Teddy Roosevelt arrives in Las Cruces via Santa Fe Railroad (with R.L. Young)

tioned earlier, Teddy Roosevelt's memories of the
Spanish American War had led him to observe, "... as
Arizona and New Mexico have not any senators and
congressmen and as I raised three-fourths of my regiment in Arizona and New Mexico, I will take their place
. . . I want to see they get a fair deal." However, it was
difficult over time for New Mexicans to see concrete evidence of his assistance. Congressional leaders continued
to concede that Arizona and New Mexico had been in
territorial status longer than any other area. However,
they rationalized their inactivity by citing the area's arid-
ity and the fact that New Mexico would be the first territory to be granted statehood in which the majority of
its inhabitants would be neither English speaking nor
Protestant. Again, in 1904, there was still another futile
attempt to gain admission of New Mexico and Arizona
as one state, with names such as Irriga and Montezuma
suggested.

Of course, there was nowhere near unanimity on the
statehood question among New Mexicans. Advocates
tended to be sophisticated Hispanics, tired of having
Washington name eastern political hacks and recent
arrivals to top administrative posts. They believed statehood would mean New Mexicans could choose their
own as leaders. Opponents feared higher taxes, public
education which would squeeze out all parochial and private schooling, an influx of eastern land grabbers and
power falling into the hands of the "wrong" party.

Anticipating that the statehood goal must surely soon
be achieved, Albert Fall made a dramatic but very
uncharacteristic move. He was well aware not only that
his Democratic party had traditionally opposed statehood but also that national and regional political trends
of the day indicated continuing Republican dominance.
This meant, in turn, that only Republican candidates

were likely to win the first two U. S. Senate seats which came with statehood. Fall had by 1904 become a Republican, explaining, "I know when to change horses."

Fall, now a newly anointed Republican, immediately went to work as an advocate of statehood. Governor Otero named him to head a delegation to Washington to lobby for statehood. In 1909, President William Howard Taft toured northern New Mexico and was honored at an elaborate banquet in Albuquerque, at which Albert Fall was featured speaker. State leaders in attendance were aghast when Fall, plain spoken as always, chided the President for foot-dragging and forgetting promises on the question of statehood. However, Taft assured the dignitaries in attendance that he would continue to support statehood and concluded his remarks with, "Judge Fall, I have heard your argument and am for your cause in spite of it." In less than a year, another Constitutional Convention was called. The constitution written in 1910 was regarded as remarkably conservative but was adopted by the electorate with a sixty percent plurality.

Statehood became official on January 6, 1912. As he signed the document naming New Mexico as the Union's forty-seventh state, President Taft remarked, "I am glad to give you life. I hope you will be healthy." The new state's first legislative session elected Thomas Catron and Albert Fall the first U. S. Senators from New Mexico. Since Catron was a former Mesillan and Fall a Las Crucen, residents of the area were elated not only over the statehood achievement but over knowing that southern New Mexico would have friendly representation in the Congress.

Chapter 7
❧ Water and the Butte ❧

The first decade of the twentieth century proved significant for Las Cruces. In 1902, leading citizens agreed
that it was time to seek territorial approval of designation of Las Cruces as an incorporated town. Walter M.
Danburg and Theodore Rouault, Jr. undertook to conduct a census, listing every resident, voter and non-voter,
adult and child and in so doing to solicit signatures of a
petition requesting the County Commission to pursue
incorporation. Doña Ana County Probate Clerk Isidoro
Armijo reported in July, 1902, that of 634 inhabitants,
181 "voters" and 81 "non-voters" had signed the petitions. Signators included many of the historically well
known names of the area-Armijo, Apodaca, Bean,
Bowman, Freudenthal, Holt, Father Lassaigne,
Llewellyn, Lohman, May, Schaublin, Schenk and thir-

teen of the nuns from Loretto Academy.

The process of winning territorial approval proved time-consuming, but it was officially incorporated as a town in 1907. Elected as trustees were Martin Lohman, the first mayor, Presiliano Moreno, Santiago P. Ascarate, Estevan Lucero, and R. L. Young. They elected R. H. Fry as Clerk. Not surprisingly, their major problem was that streets and infra-structure needed major attention, but they had no money and no taxation provision to raise money. Consequently, their first move was to issue $10,000 in bonds. They then began to establish ordinances appropriate to a newly incorporated town. For instance, they established a speed limit of six miles per hour on city streets, banned littering and spitting on sidewalks, and set a $50 fee for liquor licenses.

By the advent of statehood in 1912, the town had its first water system, charging $1.50 per month for the first 3,000 gallons with excess costing twenty cents per 1,000 gallons. They also had electric power, an ice factory, a cold storage facility, a cannery and a steam laundry. The city now had a superintendent of schools and thirteen teachers and the Loretto Academy had 150 students. Cultivated land was selling for $25 to $50 per acre and irrigation water sold for $1.25 to $2.00 per acre per year. By 1916, the town issued $20,000 in bonds to improve the water and wastewater system.

By 1913, growth was obvious. Las Cruces had six hotels. The Don Bernardo's daily rate of $2.50 was typical. The town also had two rooming houses, three banks and so many newspapers, seven, that none prospered. There were two flour mills, a canning factory, three mining companies, four oil companies, nineteen real estate agents, fourteen attorneys, nine barbers, ten physicians, two tailors, two photographers, three carpenters and five engineers. There were four general merchandise stores, seven groceries, four laundries, four blacksmiths, six livery stables, three saddlery and harness shops and one shoemaker.

It also boasted two theatres, four saloons, three drug stores, a confectionery, three restaurants, two jewelry stores, two dairies, three lumber yards, three furniture stores, two automobile agencies, three meat markets, two dry goods stores, one millinery shop, and two machine shops. There also were a plumber, a painter, an upholsterer, a cigar maker, and two undertakers. Finally, there was an implement store, a finance company, and two title and abstract offices. It also had Baptist, Catholic, Methodist and Presbyterian churches and four mission churches. A territorial post office had served the town for over sixty years, but now that it was officially a town, Capt. Thomas Branigan was postmaster from 1907 to 1912. In more recent years, the postmaster with extended years of service was Solomon Alvarez. By the advent of statehood, Doña Ana County government also was functioning well, with Felipe Lucero as sheriff and W. W. Cox serving as county treasurer. Assessed county valuation in 1907 had totalled $2,452,383, which represented one-third actual value. In 1912 the county passed a three dollar per household road tax.

Predictably, efforts now were being made to attract newcomers. Dr. Robert McBride, a physician who wore many hats, was for a time Doña Ana County's Commissioner of Immigration. The brochure he distributed bore the imposing title: *Doña Ana County in New Mexico, 1908 : Containing the Fertile Mesilla Valley, Cradle of Irrigation in America, the Garden Spot of the Great Southwest, Where Returns From the Land Are Generous and Sure.*

Dr. McBride described the Valley as including two million acres of public domain, 40,000 acres under cultivation, and another hundred thousand acres soon to be reclaimed by the Elephant Butte Irrigation Project. He assured the reader that with the rich deep soil and ideal climate, a ten acre farm would yield an independent income if "intelligently and industriously cultivated." He added, "The soil will respond with gratifying liberality to the hand of the energetic tiller ... returns are enormous in comparison with the amount of capital and labor expended." He promised a gross income of $40 to $60 per acre, with a net of $20 to $50 an acre. Even nearly a century ago, Doña Ana County farms had produced in one season 15,000 pounds of green and 4,900 pounds of red chili. McBride also noted that in 1908, the area's agriculture college boasted seven buildings and 308 students and that its Experiment Station had reported annual income of $70,000.

Dr. McBride's prediction that completion of the Elephant Butte project would bring another 100,000 acres into cultivation may have seemed overly optimistic, but Rio Grande control certainly was needed. Cycles of alternating drought and flood had bedeviled the populace and particularly farmers of the Valley for decades. Tree ring data suggested at least thirteen Rio Grande Valley droughts in the 1800s. The longest drought extended from 1894 to 1903, and in 1902 the river bed was so dry it was used as a road.

Over the years of the nineteenth and early twentieth centuries, floods were as feared as Apaches. The flood of 1865 moved the river channel from east to west of Mesilla. The flood of 1884, worst in memory, destroyed Rincon and miles of Santa Fe Railroad track, plus box cars and engines. In addition, there were floods in 1886, 1891, 1897, 1903, 1904, 1907 and 1909. In one season, Mesilla farmers had to repair flood-caused damage to their irrigation system thirteen times. By 1888 agitation for a dam to control these cycles became strident. Of course, the more obvious benefit of winning control of the grand river would be to bring life-giving water to the vast acres of potentially fertile land in the southwest.

The need for a dependable source of irrigation water had, of course, been evident ever since the founding of Las Cruces. The first task of founders in 1849 had been to dig the *acequia madre* . In the early years, volunteers assumed responsibility for ditch maintenance but it soon became clear that such an essential task required a more formal organization. A review of the rosters of ditch commissioners reveals the names of the prominent leaders of the town. By the1880s, this ditch maintenance task was the province of the Las Cruces Ditch Company with seven commissioners each from Las Cruces and Mesilla. In 1887, Martin Amador, Simon Newcomb and Jacob Schaublin were ditch commissioners and Barbaro Lucero was *mayor domo* (chairman).

Nevertheless, there was general agreement that a larger dam-controlled system must be developed. Because of these obvious needs, several proposals and schemes surfaced around the turn of the century. During 1887 and 1888 John B. Bowman, aided by Simon B. Newcomb, proposed irrigating the entire ninety mile length of the Jornada del Muerto. They claimed they could divert the Rio Grande by digging a gigantic canal from below Socorro, down the Jornada, all the way to a point below El Paso. Proposed to be eighty feet wide, ten feet deep, and two hundred miles long, the canal would cost fifteen million dollars. Of course, there was not enough water, even in flood times, to fill such a canal, nor was there enough money in Doña Ana County or the whole territory to finance such a project.

When Bowman and Newman called an El Paso public meeting to solicit support for this plan, which they promised would convert the Rio Grande into the "Nile of

America," they received verbal support but no cash. When they carried the plan to business leaders of Las Cruces, however, several thousand dollars were subscribed. Bowman then went to Washington and actually had bills introduced in both Houses of Congress to support his projected Jornada and El Paso Reservoir and Canal Company. About this time, Mesilla Valley farmers, wary of such a grandiose scheme, developed a much smaller scale canal system just below Ft. Selden. Bowman's backers began to defect and the congressional bills died in committee.

Promoter of the next water scheme was Dr. Nathan Boyd, a wealthy ex-Virginian who had bought the Dripping Springs Ranch in the Organ Mountains. He soon learned that not only were Mesilla Valley farmers deploring the effect of floods, droughts and unreliable supplies of irrigation water, but Mexican farmers south of El Paso were complaining bitterly over their lack of water. In 1888 Col. Anson Mills, an El Paso pioneer, had called for construction of a dam just north of El Paso. The probability that such a dam might materialize increased when in 1894 Colonel Mills was named U. S Commissioner on the newly established International Boundary Commission.

Sensing that El Paso might win the dam building race and, in so doing, flood 40,000 acres of fertile New Mexico farm land, Dr. Boyd determined to pursue a dam-building project. When he failed in efforts to attract investors in New Mexico, he went to England where he secured commitments of more than one and one half million dollars from English businessmen. The English backers planned to invest in American farm land, and Boyd convinced them the dam he proposed to build at Engle, more than a hundred miles north of the proposed El Paso site, would provide them with ample irrigation water.

Boyd then formed the Rio Grande Dam and Irrigation Company and in 1895 secured a construction permit from the U. S. Secretary of the Interior, providing the dam was to be completed within five years. The English then bought out Boyd, reorganized under British law, added Limited to the company name and hired Albert Fall to provide legal counsel. Farmers would pay for their irrigation water not only by forfeiting half their land to the company but also by paying a perpetual rent.

Spurred by Colonel Mills' activism, the International Boundary Commission again recommended building a dam at El Paso and managed to secure an injunction halting the British consortium's Engle Dam plans. In the next counter move, Albert Fall convinced U. S. courts that since the Rio Grande was not really navigable, in the normal sense of the word, permission to build the dam need not and should not depend upon federal government approval.

The key step toward resolving the stalemate and achieving river control was taken by the federal government. In 1902 the U. S. Reclamation Act was passed, committing the government to providing a controlled water supply in order to reclaim semi-arid and arid lands in sixteen western states and territories, including New Mexico. The act created a Reclamation Service which in 1903 quickly forfeited the British Company's franchise. It then was determined that the Bureau of Reclamation, in cooperation with the Boundary Commission, would build the dam at Engle.

A planning meeting was held in 1904, chaired by Hiram Hadley in his role as President of the Las Cruces Chamber of Commerce. It was explained that the dam should provide irrigation water for Mesilla Valley, El

Early work on Elephant Butte Dam, 1911.

Paso Valley and Juarez farmers. This was expected to provide irrigation for 180,000 acres and to cost $7,200,000, or $40 per acre. Farmers formed a water users association to collect the $40 per acre per year fee and, hopefully, repay the debt in ten years. Farmers pledged their irrigated land as a lien. Mesilla Valley farmers guaranteed more than 110,000 acres, the El Paso Valley farmers 70,000 acres and Mexican farmers were to receive 60,000 acre feet free. As it turned out, fifty-five years passed after completion of the dam before the debt was completely paid off in 1971.

In December, 1904, by-laws and articles of incorporation were drafted for what originally was called the Elephant Butte Water Users Association. H. B. Holt was named president, Oscar Snow vice president and Henry Bowman treasurer, all for six year terms. Elephant Butte Dam, so named because an island in the lake created by the dam resembled a kneeling elephant was authorized in 1907. Construction began in 1911. The nearly five year construction project involved remarkable engineering feats. Heavy equipment was brought to the small rail town of Engle, from which it had to be moved nine miles to the dam site. At its peak, the project employed 700 men. The 306 foot high dam was 1674 feet long and at its base 228 feet thick. The huge construction project was completed in 1916, creating what at that time was the world's largest man-created reservoir.

It did, however, take Valley farmers a shakedown period to efficiently benefit from the new dam's water supply. At first, farmers tended to reason that they now had an unlimited water supply, so the more used the better. Not only was over-irrigation common but poor drainage caused some soils to become alkali-encrusted in a few years. By 1920, more than a million dollars had been spent on drains, and land levelling cost farmers as much as $40 an acre.

In 1917, the Elephant Butte Irrigation District (EBID) was formed and in 1924 a congressional fact-finding committee recommended extending repayment contracts from ten to forty years and switching the obligation from individual farmers to the new EBID. Over time other improvements were effected. Five diversion dams were built, ditches were extended and maintained, and in 1938 Caballo Dam was built about twenty-five miles downstream from Elephant Butte. Caballo, ninety-seven feet high and nearly a mile long, was designed to save winter runoff and catch Black Range flood water. By January, 1946, thirty years after completion, it was estimated the entire Elephant Butte project had cost well over $21 million.

Although the federal government tried to limit EBID-involved farm sizes to 160 acres to discourage land speculation, promoters such as Nathan Boyd soon moved to profit from the planned dam. Scarcely a month after Elephant Butte Water Users had incorporated, Boyd had opened a Mesilla Valley Real Estate Company office in the Murphy building on Main Street. James

Island for which Elephant Butte Dam and Lake were named.

Sattley was president and he and his brother Clyde each contributed $10,000. Realtor James Mitchell was secretary and Boyd, developer Nicholas Galles and George Wilson served as board members. The Sattleys brought wealth to the operation because their father and uncle owned an Illinois company which had perfected the first riding plow and an experimental three-wheeled plow. In 1916 Montgomery Wards bought the farm equipment under the "Hummer" trade name.

Prices for fertile, cultivated farmlands that sold for $20 to $40 an acre in 1904, doubled by 1908 and rose to an average of $50 per acre by 1915. Another effect was the tendency of long-time resident farmers to sell their land to newcomers, so that by the time the dam was built, well over half the cultivated farm land had changed hands at least once.

As farmers adapted to their new circumstances, cotton replaced alfalfa as the cash crop of choice. It was not planted in the Valley until 1919 but by 1930 the majority of the irrigated land was in cotton. Long term hopes for agricultural benefits from the Elephant Butte system appear to have been realized, as in the 1990s, Doña Ana

✂ Water and the Butte ✂

County led the state in income from cotton, vegetables, pecans and in overall farm income.

In 1971, the Bureau of Reclamation and the irrigation district signed a document stating the district had paid off its debt to the project, but in 1997 the U. S. Interior Department filed suit seeking title to all the water in the system and claiming EBID payments bought the irrigation system and the right to operate it but not the water. Litigation on this matter of water ownership still is pending. Meanwhile, the EBID has become a 133,000 acre irrigation project, including 600 miles of canals and laterals and 400 miles of drains. In the 1960s the Soil Conservation Service added another twenty-seven flood control dams up and down the Valley.

Completed Elephant Butte Dam, 1916.

Chapter 8
❧ Banking and Growth ❧

For decades before the completion of the Elephant Butte project and certainly in the years following, agriculture was the Mesilla Valley's major industry and largest employer. The Immigration Commission advertised "Honest, industrious, thrifty immigrants are needed in Doña Ana County, men who know how and are not afraid or ashamed to work will find an inviting field and a warm welcome here." Such publications always stressed the Mesilla Valley's fortunate blend of temperate climate and rich soil and soon were praising the facts that cotton, chile, pecans and lettuce, as well as alfalfa, could be considered "year round" crops.

By 1880, farmers and ranchers began to think in terms of mutual assistance organizations. A committee formed in 1887 to plan the first county fair and the first fair opened in September of that year. In 1883, thirty cattle growers banded together to form the Doña Ana County Stock Growers, with George Lynch as president and Albert Fountain as vice president. William Rynerson served as vice president of a territory-wide Stock Growers Association. In 1889 a Doña Ana County Farmers Association formed.

Within a year after completion of the Dam the Doña Ana County Farm Bureau had been founded and, in fact, shared office space with the Elephant Butte Irrigation District in a Griggs Avenue building called the Temple of Agriculture. For some years in the more recent past, the building housed the Gospel Rescue Mission. In mid-1998, the Farm Bureau moved into a large modern building on north Telshor Boulevard.

Only a few of the many Mesilla Valley agricultural leaders who contributed to the Valley's developing farming industry can be credited in a book such as this, but some must be mentioned. For instance, Oscar Snow, a member of New Mexico A. & M.'s first graduating class in 1894, started purchasing farm land while still in college and by the early 1900s had accumulated eleven hundred acres south of Las Cruces, all planted in alfalfa. He became known as "Alfalfa King" of the Valley, although he also experimented with wheat and milo and planted walnut and persimmon trees.

Theodore Rouault, a native Frenchman, came to the valley in 1879. Starting in the hardware business, in which he was involved for over thirty years, he soon was growing fruit, including grapes, chiles, tomatoes and other vegetables, which supplied his canning plant and winery-distillery. He served two terms as County Assessor and took a great interest in securing quality education for the county's children.

Thomas Casad was born in Ohio of French parentage but devoted his life to farming and sheep raising. Soon after he arrived in Mesilla in 1874, he bought over ten thousand acres of the Brazito Land Grant from Hugh Stevenson. He initially grew fruit and grapes but soon converted to alfalfa, plus stocking his farm with pure-bred Angora goats and Poland China hogs. He also operated a flour mill.

Benjamin E. Davies arrived in the Valley with the California Column. He soon started acquiring cattle and sheep, including some blooded breeds. In time, he was able, in partnership with Morris Lesinsky, to buy the Shedd Ranch in the foothills of the Organ Mountains. By 1882, he had ten thousand sheep and became one of the most knowledgeable sheepmen in New Mexico. However, by 1885, he introduced blooded Hereford cattle and began to concentrate on cattle. He helped organize and served as president of the Doña Ana County Stock Association. After Davies' death, the ranch was sold to Numa Reymond.

In 1893, William W. (W. W.) Cox bought the ranch. Like Davies, he initially stocked it with sheep but soon concluded, as Davies had, that sheep tended to destroy pasture and cattle growing was better for semi-desert country. In time he controlled 150,000 acres, one of the largest ranches in southern New Mexico. In 1945, the U. S. Army bought ninety percent of the ranch, but the Cox family still owns and occupies the ranch house.

Francis C. Barker came to the Valley from England as a tubercular health seeker in 1885. He started farming on two acres near the Santa Fe depot and by 1895 added thirty more acres in order to specialize in asparagus. His son, Percy W., got a degree in business and took over management of the Barker Farms. Specializing in vegetable farming, he was considered the first scientific farmer in the Southwest.

❧ Banking and Growth ❧

Seeking a healthy clime for his tubercular wife, as well as news of the Elephant Butte Dam, brought the Frank Archer family from Alabama to the San Miguel area, south of Las Cruces, in 1920. Archer had farmed cotton in Alabama and soon was one of the earliest cotton farmers of this area, hauling bales by wagon to the Anderson Clayton gin in Las Cruces. Of five Archer sons, three of them, Walter, Ben and Julius became prominent in the Hatch-Rincon area. Walter served a term as Doña Ana County Commissioner. Ben served as County Treasurer and mayor of Hatch. He also was instrumental in founding of the Health Centers at Hatch, Truth or Consequences and north Las Cruces which bear his name.

Jacob Schaublin, a Swiss immigrant, settled in Las Cruces in 1860. He dabbled in mining to the point where he could afford to invest in Valley land and developed a large vineyard and orchard. This led, in turn, to his becoming one of the largest wine makers in the Valley. Schaublin was elected County School Commissioner in 1880 and was appointed to New Mexico A. & M.'s first Board of Regents.

In 1882 he further diversified, buying the El Molino flour mill, which could produce ten thousand pounds of flour a day. That mill was built in 1847 on the banks of the *acequia madre* near the present site of the First National (Security) Bank. Don Salvador Cordova was owner of the site and builder of the mill. The mill almost immediately prospered, at times employing six men and producing 100 sacks in twenty-four hours. It nevertheless changed ownership frequently in the early years. Thomas Bull and James Harris bought it, but in turn sold to Susanne Draper, who established it as Draper's Mill and Gardens. Subsequent owners included Emil Conway, Louise Topley, Lloyd Hufstedter, Gerald

Keaton, Gustav and Numa Granjean and Henry
Lesinsky, who kept Numa Granjean as his miller.
Lesinsky sold to the above mentioned Jacob Schaublin,
who renovated the mill and the garden and added a
warehouse with capacity for 25,000 bushels of grain.

The Schaublin enterprise fell victim to another of the
periodic droughts. In 1879, the *acequia* ran dry, the village of Doña Ana dammed the river and Las Crucens
damned Doña Ana. The price of flour skyrocketed.
Since the Santa Fe Railroad had not yet reached southern New Mexico it was difficult to secure wheat or flour
from outside sources. Undaunted and unwilling to vic-
timize local farmers, Schaublin sold all his stored wheat
at nominal prices and ordered a twenty horse power
steam engine so as to resume mill operation. However,
the drought ended and it is believed the steam engine
never was used. Soon after 1900 the mill was abandoned, except as storage for merchandise from Martin
Lohman's store.

In 1939 Louise Topley and her children, Bruce and
Phyllis, opened one of the area's first motels, the El
Molino, and an adjacent restaurant, on the site where the
mill had stood. Early in 1960, the Cruces Investment
Company, of which Frank O. Papen was board chair-
man, bought the motel and restaurant with a view to
eventually replacing them with the Loretto Shopping
Mall in 1965 and the First National Bank Tower in 1967.

Armed conflict on two fronts intruded on southern
New Mexico soon after completion of the Elephant
Butte project. Because revolutionary violence had waxed
and waned in Mexico since 1910, the United States had
stationed 350 soldiers, including nearly thirty college students, at the town of Columbus, on the border south of
Deming. On March 9, 1916, Mexico's Col. Pancho Villa
led his revolutionary troops across the border to burn

and loot Columbus. Seventeen Americans, including
New Mexico A. & M. graduate Charles D. Miller were
killed (Appendix 7 of this volume lists the men who
served when local national guard units were activated.)

The U. S. armed garrison at Columbus soon was in
hot but futile pursuit of the Villistas. Gen. John J.
Pershing then was named to command a Punitive
Expedition to capture Villa. As the nearest town of any
size, Las Cruces frequently played host to troops in transit or on leave. Nearly twenty years after his disappoint-
ingly inactive military service in the Spanish American
War, Albert Fall offered to resign from the Senate. He
proposed to raise as many as three regiments to fight
Villa. His proposal was conditioned on his being
appointed commanding officer and given free rein to, if
necessary, occupy all of northern Mexico. Again, Fall's
combative ambitions went unfulfilled. After nearly a year
in Mexico without apprehending Villa, American troops
were withdrawn.

Following the Villa raid, some apprehension was
expressed that Anglos might associate those who then
were called Spanish-Americans with Villista atrocities.
Attorney-banker H. B. Holt chaired a committee which
raised seven companies of home guard to protect Las
Cruces. Sheriff Felipe Lucero announced that all
"enemy aliens" were to turn in any guns, ammunition,
wireless bombs, signaling devices or code books in their
possession to his office.

Individuals and newspapers attempted, however, to
calm such fears and feelings, pointing out that many of
New Mexico's National Guardsmen were loyal Spanish-
Americans who were known for their respect for the law
and their peaceful nature. Sheriff Lucero also published
a proclamation assuring that "no citizen of any foreign
power ... should fear any invasion of his personal or

property rights...." Talk about race and loyalty issues soon diminished, especially when it became increasingly probable that the United States was destined to enter World War I.

After the U.S. declared war against Germany in April, 1917, Las Cruces mayor John May called a city holiday so all twenty-one to thirty year old males could register for the military draft. New Mexico A. & M. enrollment of course plummeted with a 1918 commencement awarding only seven degrees. The spring semester of 1918 brought news that Capt. Joseph Quesenberry had died on the Western Front, the first former Aggie to be killed in action. Because of the war, the administration compressed the 1918 spring semester into two months by scheduling classes six days a week. The military draft bedeviled male students, especially the engineers and agriculturists, uncertain as to whether they were in "preferred" or "deferred" categories. The College instituted a program called Student Army Training Corps (S. A. T. C.). However, the program was hardly operational when the war ended and it was transformed into the traditional R. O. T. C.

Las Cruces' young soldiers suffered at least their share of fatalities and disabling injuries. Survivors returned seeking land and jobs and the state did exempt wounded veterans from taxation. In addition to community concern over its sons serving in France, the community also suffered from an epidemic of what was called Spanish flu in 1918. More than 1,000 New Mexicans died, including a son and daughter of Albert Fall (then a U. S. Senator). Public schools and the college were closed during the peak of the epidemic.

Well before the nation's economic collapse in 1929, prosperity had deserted many southern New Mexicans. Elephant Butte Dam had not yet brought the anticipated prosperity and by the mid-1920s vegetable and fruit prices were plummeting and even cotton prices in 1933 were less than one-fourth their 1923 level. Because of a willingness to innovate and gamble, one family which bucked the depression trend was the Stahmanns.

W. J. Stahmann headed west from Wisconsin in 1907, seeking a healthier climate for his tubercular wife. After a stop in Arkansas, the Stahmanns moved on to Fabens, Texas. W.J. started a honey making business but soon expanded his farm operation to a cotton gin and compress and a tomato canning plant. He and his son Deane then moved to the Mesilla Valley and by 1936 Deane was farming 4,000 acres. He started with conventional cotton, fruit and vegetable crops but a bargain in pecan trees started him in a different and very profitable direction.

He planted row after row of young pecan trees and between the rows, he planted cotton and brought in geese which not only weeded and fertilized the fields but also produced marketable feathers and eggs. Eventually Stahmann farms not only became the largest pecan orchard in the world but profited from remarkably successful marketing techniques, including opening a retail and mail order outlet at the farm.

As this new century unfolded, census figures reflected a slow but steady Las Cruces population growth. The first decade of the century, growth occurred at the rate of about one hundred per year. The second (World War I) decade, growth slowed to an average of only about 15 per year. The post war decade, 1920 to 1930, brought a population spurt, reaching 5,811 and averaging a gain of nearly 200 per year (See Appendix 3). The business center was still the three or four blocks of Main Street with the same poorly maintained board sidewalks, hitching posts, and adobe and/or wooden buildings with flat roofs extending over the sidewalk to provide sun shelter in the summer heat.

While it may have been apocryphal, one historian said the period's most popular entertainment was funerals. The coffin was placed on the hearse, rented from the Women's Improvement Association, with the wheel spokes wrapped in blue calico. Mesilla's Gamboa Band, featuring its E Flat cornets, led the procession across the *acequia* bridge near the Amador Hotel. As the band marched, it played the "Mexican Quadrille" or "Dixie," depending on the status of the deceased. When the hearse reached the railroad tracks, the horses often balked until pallbearers and onlookers pushed it and its team across the rails.

With the Rio Grande controlled, agriculture relatively stable despite economic downturns, the college well established, and the variety and acumen of business ventures improving, one facet of the economic infra-structure upon which it all depended still needed to be developed and that was banking.

Efforts to provide banking-type services actually had begun more than a century ago. The first full scale bank in the New Mexico Territory, called the First National Bank, had been opened by Lucien Maxwell in Santa Fe in 1870. By May, 1881, Numa Reymond's Main Street mercantile was the first to attempt to provide financial services to his patrons, by offering use of his safe.

Later that same year, A. H. Reynolds (some sources spell the name Raynolds) opened the town's first official bank, but after only a year and a half in business, sold out in 1882 to D. M. and J. M. Evans, doing business as the Evans Brothers Bank. In 1883, after reports of possible embezzlement led to receivership, George D. Bowman and sons, George R. and Henry D., bought out the Evans' interests. In 1894, Henry Bowman bought

out his brother and in 1903 bought his father's interest.
For ten years Henry operated the Bowman Bank.
Meanwhile, new Las Cruces resident Albert Bacon Fall
joined his law partner, N. M. Lowry, in opening the Las
Cruces Building and Loan Association in 1887. Two
years later they formed a Las Cruces branch of the
American Building and Loan Association, with Phoebus
Freudenthal as president, George Bowman as treasurer
and Fall as attorney.

It soon became important that banks be legally certified as "national" banks. Only a national bank could be a
United States government depository and offer to provide permanent deposit facilities for government funds.
In those days, a national bank could print its own cur-
rency and each bill carried on its face the bank's name.
This was certainly inexpensive advertising. Federal
money would become available to local communities and
with farm land being sold and resold, demand would
increase for loans and investments.

In 1905, Bowman reorganized the Bowman Bank,
named himself president and, with businessman Henry
Stoes, applied for a national bank charter. However, promoter Nathan Boyd was still pushing Doña Ana county
development. He had what proved to be valuable backing and contacts. He arranged to have his old friend,
Clyde Sattley, then residing in Springfield, Illinois, apply
to the federal comptroller for the title "First National
Bank of Las Cruces." Charters for Bowman and Boyd's
national bank proposals arrived in the comptroller's
office on the same day, May 3, 1905. Because he had
arranged what appeared to be substantial financial backing, Boyd won the "national" charter and his First
National Bank of Las Cruces opened in the Murphy
building on Main Street on May 3, 1905. Henry
Bowman's sons continued in banking but Henry's

"national" bank never opened.

The Sattleys talked Abraham Daughenbaugh, a wealthy Iowa merchant, into financing the First National venture. Daughenbaugh, in turn, persuaded C. Fay Sperry, an Iowa banker, to bring banking expertise to the endeavor. After the bank actually opened, Daughenbaugh and Clyde Sattley vanished , without explanation, from the official records. The new bank sold 250 shares of stock at $100 per share. Of the $25,000 in stock backing the bank, Sperry was majority stockholder, with 130 of its 250 shares. Stockholders elected Nicholas Galles, Nathan Boyd, James P. Mitchell, R. M. Mayes and Sperry to the board of directors. The directors, in turn, named Galles, president; Boyd, vice president; Sperry, cashier; and Theodore Rouault, Jr., assistant cashier. New president Galles, born in Chicago, and educated in Minnesota, certainly brought a varied background to the job. He had taught school in Socorro and studied law under Albert Fountain, had served as a captain in the New Mexico Volunteer Militia and was considered one of the founders of Hillsboro.

The new board of directors announced that First National business hours would be from nine to three o'clock weekdays, nine to noon on Saturday, and that deposits would earn five percent interest. One month after opening, the board paid $5,000 for a three-quarter block 305 North Main Street tract, known as the Ochoa property. Supervised by George Stahl, construction soon began on a combination brick and adobe building, with a seventy-eight foot frontage and one hundred foot depth.

Interestingly, during excavation for the foundation of the new building, adobe buildings on both sides collapsed, but construction proceeded and it came to be known as "Banking House." Problems with completing the building may have been a forewarning of problem-filled banking business during the early years. After a little over three months of operation, concern over questionable loans and overdrafts led the directors to request and receive Nathan Boyd's resignation. Boyd then shifted his attention back to real estate, buying the Shalam Colony property, hoping but failing to develop a sanatorium. In 1918 he was again into banking, opening the Boyd Union Bank. By 1921 the Bowman Bank and the Boyd Union Bank, both struggling, merged as Bowman's Bank and Trust Company, with W. W. Cox as president, but that firm failed in 1922.

Following Boyd's departure, Captain Samuel Woodhull replaced him as vice president and director. Woodhull built the Park Hotel near Pioneer Park and by 1907 had bought and announced plans to restore what had been Dr. McBride's Alameda sanatorium. When First National's board of directors held their bylaw-required meeting in January, 1906, Oscar Snow was elected president. As successful in business and farming as Snow had been, his early presidential tenure also was plagued by overdrafts and unpaid loans. Nevertheless, he served as president of First National for over twenty years. Examiners regularly complained that the bank's greatest problem was officer and director overdrafts and one examiner said, apparently for good reason, that New Mexico had the most lax and slipshod bank laws in the United States.

After the nationwide economic slump of 1907, called the "rich man's panic," there was much shuffling of bank officials in Las Cruces and across the country. Fay Sperry resigned, but in 1911 opened a rival bank, First State Bank, which lasted less than three years. Another competitor, Farmers Trust Bank merged with First National in 1918. Meanwhile, William A. Sutherland

and H. B. Holt, law partners, successful defense attorneys, members of the New Mexico A. & M. Board of Regents and in Holt's case, a New Mexico legislator and candidate for U. S. Senate, tended to guide First National policy in the decades of the 1910s and 1920s. One concern of examiners in the pre-World War I period was possible conflict of interest between directors who also were primary stock holders of the Las Cruces Electric Light and Ice Company. Snow, Holt, Sutherland and Woodhull, all Light Company officers and/or directors, were ordered to sell their stock and the company ultimately was sold to El Paso Electric Company.

Sutherland left the Board of Directors in 1926. Holt served briefly as president of First National in 1928 after the death of Snow. He soon was replaced by William P. B. McSain who had been El Paso County Tax Assessor/Collector and Vice President and a director of El Paso National Bank. Although Holt was removed as a director in the depression-forced reorganization of 1931, he continued as legal advisor until his death in 1957.

It was McSain who guided the bank through the early depression years. As early as 1923, First National directors sensed the approach of economic hard times and ceased making loans for land investments. When the stock market crashed in 1929, McSain described First National as "absolutely solvent," but in 1931 closed its doors for fifty-five days until "the hysteria subsides." His actions were based not only on a reluctance to foreclose on property of his friends in the farming and ranching community but also on the foreknowledge that should he do so, there would be no buyers interested in or able to bid on the foreclosed property.

The bank reopened in October, 1931, with McSain replaced by A.I. Kelso, founder in 1927 and president of Mutual Building and Loan Association. McSain continued as bank manager, but died shortly after President Franklin Roosevelt ordered a national bank holiday in March, 1933. Finally, First National reopened on May 22, 1933 and has operated successfully ever since.

Kelso served the bank as president from 1931 to 1954, the longest tenure of any president. J. J. Aragon and Claud Tharp each held the position for three years. Frank O. Papen served from 1971 to 1982 and again from 1982 to 1987. Charles Haner served between the two Papen terms and Papen then was succeeded by Ben Haines.

Papen, often referred to as Mr. First National, came to Las Cruces from Las Vegas, New Mexico, in 1940 and partnered with Frank Weisenhorn in an insurance agency. Aided by the organizational and managerial skills of his wife, Julie, Frank turned Weisenhorn-Papen into the largest insurance agency in New Mexico. Weisenhorn had joined the First National board of direc-

Dedication of Doña Ana County Courthouse (1937 or 1938).
Photographer is former Gov. James F. Hinkle.

tors in 1938 and in 1952 Papen also was elected to the First National board.

Papen became increasingly frustrated at the conservative, cautious approach First National took to growth and modernization. Las Cruces had expanded into a town of 30,000 people but residents usually tended to shop in El Paso and farmers and businessmen borrowed from El Paso banks. Papen turned the bank into an expansion and consumer oriented institution which aggressively offered installment loans. By 1955 he was on a committee which recommended leasing a lot for drive-in facilities, in 1958 established a trust department, and soon expanded to Anthony and White Sands Missile Range.

One key to Frank Papen's managerial success was his ability to recruit assistants whose talents matched the needs of the bank. A prime example was his persuading General Hugh M. Milton to join the First National team in 1961. Milton, born and educated in Kentucky, had joined the mechanical engineering faculty at New Mexico A. & M. in 1924 after first teaching at Texas A. & M. From then on his career had been one of consistent advancement. By 1933 he had become the College's dean of engineering and in 1938 was named college president. World War II duty interrupted and Milton advanced to the rank of brigadier general, was chief of staff for the XIV Corps in the South Pacific and entered the Philippines with Gen. Douglas MacArthur. After the war he served as president of the New Mexico Military Institute at Roswell until President Eisenhower called him back to Washington to serve as Assistant Secretary of the Army in 1953. By 1958 he had advanced to Under Secretary of the Army.

When General Milton left Washington in 1961, he joined Papen's staff as vice president in charge of public relations. He had a persuasive voice, ingratiating smile, strong hand shake and commanding presence and was, as one future successor to his job said, "the right man with the right skills at the right time." His eleven years at First National came when improving public relations was perhaps the bank's greatest need and he met that need admirably.

Frank Papen served his community in many ways. He served for ten years in the New Mexico House of Representatives and then several terms in the New Mexico Senate. He served for a time as chairman of the Las Cruces Chamber of Commerce, as president of the New Mexico State University Foundation and in many civic roles. As a state senator he assisted Senator Lamar Gwaltney in the legislative fight to win approval of state funds to aid construction of the university's 31,000 seat football stadium in 1978.

Meanwhile, Patterson Fitzgerald Campbell, another health-seeking tubercular immigrant, arrived in Las Cruces from Mississippi in 1909. He soon gained

Dedication of El Molino Grinding Stone, First National Bank
L to R: Hugh Milton, Charles Haner, Robert Munson, Frank Papen.

employment as cashier at First National Bank. In 1914, the Bank of Hatch opened and Campbell became vice president-cashier. By 1917 it was well established with 150 individual depositors as well as major fluorspar mining company business depositors. However, a nation-wide recession and the collapse of the mining venture in 1920, were followed by a disastrous 1921 Placitas Arroyo flood which destroyed the bank, Campbell's home and much of the town. The multiple disasters caused Campbell to give up on Hatch banking.

Back in Las Cruces, he became acquainted with the Valley's most successful scientific farmer, Percy Barker. By 1922, the two had established the Mesilla Valley Bank, with Barker as president and Campbell as cashier and directors W. O. Hall, Ben Luchini, Frank Herron, Campbell and Barker. As the city's second financial institution, the bank quickly proved successful and boasted that it had not a single default during the depression.

By the late 1950s, Campbell had retired and both he and Barker had died. Barker's son, Arthur, took over the bank but it became as self-satisfied and conservative as the pre-Papen First National. Former Texan, Lawrence Walker, manager of insurance and cotton companies, bought the bank, became its president and renamed it Farmers and Merchants Bank. Under a board of directors including Walter Archer, Rufus Garland, Lamar Gwaltney, Seaborn Collins, Dr. C. S. Carver, J. B. Harris , Santos Lara and Gen. F. H. Tenney, the bank aggressively sought to serve community financial and lending needs and it steadily progressed. In 1971, Dallas A. Johnson became president and chief executive officer and in 1978 it changed its name to Western Bank. Present president is Bill Robertson.

The success and apparent stability of First National and Farmers and Merchants/Western attracted competition. In 1970, J. A. Ikard and his sons, John and Jim, renovated and preserved many of the historic features of the old Amador Hotel and established Citizen's Bank. An effort was made to display as many as possible of the old Amador historic artifacts. Its first president was Isidoro Armijo and the board of directors included Judge Edward Triviz, home builders Carlos Blanco and Lewis Emerick and businessmen John and Jim Ikard. Current president is Justin Harper.

An interesting link to the Catholic Church then dramatically affected all three of the city's financial institutions. It started when Frank Papen learned that Bishop Sidney Metzger had decided to demolish historic but obsolete and deteriorating St. Genevieve's church and to rebuild on the site of Loretto Academy at the south end of Main Street. Papen, frustrated that there was no room for First National to expand at its 301 North Main Street site, contracted to buy the St. Genevieve's site. He had not, however, anticipated the emotional public outcry which greeted the news of St. Genevieve's planned demise. As the outcry grew, it was decided to concentrate instead on the Loretto Academy site. It developed that once St. Genevieve's had been demolished, despite protests, the urban renewal program converted the site to a parking lot. Western Bank soon after purchased the property and built a four-story headquarters building on that block of the Downtown Mall.

In 1962, First National moved into its new facility, graced by beautiful Manuel Acosta murals, and modified its name to First National Bank of Doña Ana County. Papen also arranged purchase of the Gallagher house (until recently the Bates law firm) and El Molino Courts and restaurant, preparatory to construction of Loretto Shopping Mall, the first enclosed, air-cooled retail center in New Mexico, which opened in 1965. Finally, Papen realized a long-held dream and erected the ten story First National Tower, a nearly two million dollar project which opened in 1967. Some measure of the growth of First National under Frank Papen's guidance is revealed in total asset statistics. In 1957, assets totalled $9,595,000. By mid-1990, they totalled nearly $307,000,000.

The third bank to locate on what once was historically Catholic church-owned property was the city's largest currently home-owned and operated bank, Citizens. After nearly two decades at the Amador site, it remodeled the old Loretto Shopping Center, once the site of Loretto Academy, converting it to an upscale office center called Loretto Towne Center and located its extensive main bank facility there. In 1998, Citizen's Bank is undergoing extensive remodeling which will be designed to facilitate display of many more Amador Hotel artifacts which have been in storage.

A nation-wide trend to bank mergers and holding companies, exemplified by the recent merger of Norwest Bank and Wells Fargo, has affected both pioneer Las Cruces banking institutions. Western has been acquired by Community First Bancshares of North Dakota and is now named Community First Bank. First National became the property of a holding company, Rio Grande Bankshares, which in turn became part of First Security Corporation. It has, in 1998 formally changed its name from First National to First Security Bank.

As Las Cruces prepares to celebrate its one hundred fiftieth anniversary, it now boasts thirteen banks plus a recently opened banking institution in Mesilla. First National (Security) now has nine branches plus a mortgage loan branch and Citizens and Western (Community First) each have several branches and/or drive up facilities. In addition to First Security, Community First and

❦ Banking and Growth ❦

Citizens, there are Bank of America, Bank of New
Mexico, Bank of the Rio Grande, First Federal, First
Savings, Matrix Capital, Nations, Norwest, Pioneer,
Sierra, and Mesilla's First National. The city also has
two depositor-owned federal credit unions, White Sands
and Fort Bliss, each of which operates branches.

Chapter 9
❧ Successful Families ❧

It is impossible to include biographical sketches of all the outstanding individuals and families who have significantly contributed to Las Cruces' development, so the author has included a representative sampling, with apologies to the many equally deserving names which may seem to be overlooked.

Pennsylvanian John Lemon, referred to in earlier chapters, learned the freighting business from an uncle. After trips to Oregon and living in California, he moved to Mesilla in 1860, opened a mercantile store and freighted goods to Forts Selden, Craig and Cummings. His customers included Col. Kit Carson, General James Carleton, Judge Roy Bean, and the Rynersons and Bennetts. Lemon's business success was interrupted, however, by Confederate occupation of Mesilla. Because he refused to support or cooperate with Confederate Colonel Baylor, he was arrested, jailed, had his property seized and came near to being hanged.

Lemon was an active parishioner and supporter of San Albino church and worked with William Rynerson to build the local Republican party. He was county probate judge from 1864-1869 and then was Deputy Collector of United State Customs in Las Cruces and Customs Inspector in Mesilla. On the day of the 1871 Mesilla riot, the Republican rally was held at the Lemon home. The spark which led to fatal violence came when the Republican rally broke up and Lemon led them to enjoy one last march around Mesilla's plaza. John Lemon was the first fatality.

Henry Boyer was born in Georgia, taken west to Missouri, and later became a teamster/wagoner for the U.S. Army in the Mexican War. He was with Colonel Doniphan at the battle of Brazito. The youngest of Henry's eight children was Frank, who became a skilled debater at Atlanta's Morehouse College and worked as a proof reader at the Atlanta *Constitution*.

After he taught school for several years, Frank and two friends spent 1899 walking 2,000 miles to Roswell, New Mexico. He worked as a cook and ranch hand in the Roswell-Dexter area and as soon as he was able to homestead 160 acres, his wife, father and seven children joined him. After unsuccessful attempts to establish a black community in southeast New Mexico, the Boyers packed all their possessions in six wagons and moved on to the Mesilla Valley and the town of Vado (The Spanish word vado means "ford.") Frank amassed 500 acres of farm land and a thriving community developed, based largely on cotton farming. He was directly responsible for forty to sixty families settling in Vado between 1922 and 1935.

Doña Ana County Sheriff Felipe Lucero, Deputies Bob Burch and
Morgan Llewellyn, Church Street.

Frank took the lead in building a one-room adobe
school house and the Valley Grove Baptist Church. At
that time, the 1925 New Mexico school law mandated
public school segregation and even after the New
Mexico legislature officially abolished segregation in the
mid-1950s, scattered instances of school segregation persisted until 1967. When the Ku Klux Klan burned a
cross in Vado, Frank Boyer petitioned for and secured
establishment of Paul Lawrence Dunbar School in Vado.
For some years, however, Vado's black children were
transported to Las Cruces' Booker T. Washington
School in Gadsden School District buses. Frank also
instigated the formation of a Vado Town Council and
was instrumental in forming the Valley Grove Masonic
Lodge. Frank's family has continued his devotion to
community and education. By 1988, Frank's great grandson, Mitchell, served a four year term on the Gadsden
school board, including one year as president.

Isabel Lucero Beckett, born in 1918 in Las Cruces,
was descended from Pedro Lucero Godoy who arrived
in Santa Fe from Mexico City in 1617. Her great grand-

father, Don Barbaro Lucero, was a teamster for Maj. W. H. Emory and the United States-Mexico Border Commission. He was in Mesilla in 1854 when the Gadsden Purchase signing was celebrated. He moved to Mesilla in 1859 and farmed near Picacho, raising grain for army posts. Barbaro's brother, Juan, formed a freighting company and made annual six to seven month round trips to St. Louis and back to Las Cruces. His company consisted of ten wagons, each drawn by ten oxen and on one trip his wagons were part of a caravan of 300 men, 150 wagons and 2,000 animals.

Francisco, Barbaro's eldest son, was killed by Apaches while engaged in freighting near Lordsburg. Two other sons, Jose and Felipe, served in Doña Ana County elective positions for more than thirty-five years. They alternated as sheriff or deputy beginning with the election of 1900, when Jose defeated Pat Garrett, to 1922 and again in 1925-1928 and 1935-1936 (See Appendix # 1). In addition, Jose served a term as Doña Ana county clerk and a six year term as a New Mexico A. and M. College regent. They were the only sheriffs with official Mexican authorization to pursue fugitives into Mexico. Barbaro and both Jose and Felipe ranched in the White Sands area. Lucero School was named for the family and the land on which the Union High School (now the state judicial complex) was erected was owned by them and given to the city. Two of the descendants of the Luceros are Archie and Pat Beckett, who are local historians and writers. Pat is owner of the Coas book stores and Archie was named to the Doña Ana County Historical Society's Hall of Fame for 1998 for his work as a founder of the city's Oral History Club.

Julius Freudenthal arrived in the United States in 1856 from Prussia. His nephew, Henry Lesinsky, after a failed 1857 search for gold in California, joined his uncle

in 1859 in opening a mercantile establishment in La
Mesa, south of Las Cruces. A year later they moved the
store to Las Cruces. One of Julius' sons, Morris, worked
in the family's mercantile business until 1899 when he
bought the Armijo home on North Main and converted
it into the Don Bernardo Hotel.

Another son of Julius, Phoebus, joined the family
business in 1870. He helped open Lesinsky stores in El
Paso and Silver City. When Numa Reymond bought out
Lesinsky, he helped Phoebus establish his own store in
Las Cruces. Phoebus built the first brick building in Las
Cruces. He was president of the local Farm Bureau,
served two terms as county treasurer, and was Treasurer
and then a member of the Board of Regents at New
Mexico A. & M. In 1899, Phoebus moved to
Solomonville, in eastern Arizona, to open a store there.

Louis, Phoebus' son, was a seven year old when his
parents moved to Arizona but he opted to stay in Las
Cruces, living at the Don Bernardo Hotel with his uncle
Morris and Aunt Minna. He graduated with a degree in
Agriculture from Cornell University and returned to
manage Freudenthal farms in the Valley. He developed
the first system of rack drying of onions and was a pio-
neer in delivering fresh eggs to local residents. He was
an arid lands specialist, state president of the Farm
Bureau and was an advocate of a program such as the
Civilian Conservation Corps, later adopted by President
Franklin Roosevelt. In 1918 he started the Valley
Insurance Agency, which specialized in financing farm-
ing endeavors. He also was a fine classical pianist and he
and Adlai Feather were founders of the Doña Ana
County Historical Society (See Appendix 9 for Hall of
Fame Honorees.)

When Louis had returned from Cornell University to
Las Cruces, he owned one of the town's earliest Ford

cars. In those days service stations were rare and drivers had to carry tools and supplies with them and serve as their own mechanic. Paved roads were non-existent. It was not until the 1920s that concrete paving came into use and then it was laid down in large blocks. Louis left a diary account of a wild trip he made with two visiting students from South Africa. They traveled to Deming, Lordsburg, Solomonville and Globe, Arizona, and even on to Roosevelt Dam on the Apache Trail.

New Mexico's territorial government had called a Good Roads Convention in 1904, attended by several Doña Ana County delegates. The county then appointed precinct road commissioners whose orders that road blocking fences had to go and bridges had to be repaired were to be enforced by justices of the peace. Precincts were urged to make every effort to get road work done on a voluntary basis. In 1908, Las Cruces held its own Good Roads Convention attended by two hundred people. That same year, the first Model T Ford appeared in town, owned by the Brown Realty Company. In 1909 a Territorial Road Commission was created and $5,000 was appropriated to the superintendent of the state prison for convict road work. It is believed the first paved road (1923) in Las Cruces was Depot Road (now Las Cruces Avenue) extending from Main Street to the Santa Fe Depot. It was not until 1928 that the Las Cruces town board passed an ordinance providing for street lighting.

Louis' wife, Carmen, was president of the Women's Improvement Association in 1940 and worked for thirty-two years to improve her adopted community. She championed community property rights for women, established a prenatal and well baby clinic, formed the hospital auxiliary, helped open Planned Parenthood clinics, was a child labor law activist and helped organize the

annual Community Concert series. Their daughter, Elsa
Freudenthal Altshool, has continued the family tradition
of community activism and contributions.

One of Las Cruces' oldest still occupied residences
(until recently a law office) is historically known as the
Armijo-Gallagher house. Mariano Samaniego, first
known owner of the property, sold it in 1867 to John
D. Barncastle, son-in-law of Las Cruces founder Pablo
Melendres for $160. In a little over a year, Barncastle
sold the property for $2,000 to Mrs. Bradford
(Marriosita) Daily. Her husband had worked as a scout
and spy for the Union army and then became active and
successful in the freighting business, although he was
often victimized by Apache raids.

Bradford Daily died in 1875 and in 1877 Nestor
Armijo acquired the property, one and one-half acres
and a four room adobe house with three foot thick walls,
for $4,050. Armijo had been a Santa Fe Trail trader in
his teens and while travelling with his father, happened
to pass through Doña Ana in 1849 when residents were
drawing lots for the newly platted Las Cruces town site.
He made considerable money driving large herds of
sheep from El Paso to Yuma, then began a trading business between Missouri and Chihuahua, which facilitated
his opening mercantile stores in Las Cruces and El Paso.
He used ten-mule schooner wagons, each capable of carrying two to three tons of merchandise valued at
$150,000. Armijo shifted his business base to Chihuahua
in 1868, but Mexican revolutionary violence led him
back to Las Cruces in 1872. He acquired large tracts of
land and invested in an Organ Mountain mine with
Colonel Rynerson, while continuing his mercantile and
freight business. He left an estate of nearly 1.5 million
dollars and was listed by the 1900 census as a capitalist.

Nestor Armijo became one of Doña Ana County's

richest men and thus was able to turn the Daily property into a community showplace. The remodeling added a second story, probably the first two-story building in town, and four additional bedrooms. The four poster brass English-made bed bought in Chihuahua was so high the ceiling of the second floor bedroom had to be raised. Hand carved limestone *canales* (channels) drained water from the roof. It later became the first Las Cruces home to have electricity. The house also was occupied by Don Nestor's son Carlos and later by grand daughter Josefa and her husband Peter Gallagher, explaining the publicly used name Armijo-Gallagher house. Five Armijo generations were reared in the house.

Located at East Lohman and South Main, adjacent to the Citizens Bank-Loretto Towne Center complex, the integrity of the old house was conserved by Pioneer Savings and Loan when it opened its branch office there in 1982. More recently it has been the Law Office of Lloyd Bates. In the ten years he occupied the building, Bates made every effort to maintain and preserve its historic features, but in mid-1998, the law office was moved

Armijo-Gallagher home, north of Loretto Towne Center, 150 E. Lohman.

and the Armijo-Gallagher house, currently owned by Citizens Bank, is unoccupied.

It should be noted that Armijo Street was named for another Armijo, Jacinto. What now is Armijo Street originally ran through what was the Armijo ranch east of Water Street. Jacinto Armijo served as a New Mexico A. & M. regent, Doña Ana County commissioner, territorial legislator, school trustee and probate judge. It was Jacinto Armijo who joined the triumvirate of Rynerson, Newcomb, and Cuniffe in the Las Cruces Town Company development. It was they who platted the old Armijo ranch into lots and donated land for the Santa Fe right of way and depot. Sometimes referred to as the new addition, it extended north to south from Mountain Avenue to Amador and east to west from Water Street to the railroad.

Thomas Branigan was born in Scotland but his family migrated to Ohio when he was two years old. At the age of fourteen, upon the outbreak of the Civil War, he joined the Ohio Volunteers and fought in the Union Army for three years. He then worked as a buffalo hunter, gold prospector, stagecoach driver, railroad bridge builder, cattle farmer, prison guard and railroad detective. In 1882, he accepted a job as Captain and Chief of Scouts at the Mescalero Apache Reservation. While there he struck up a friendship with Mescalero Indian Agent William H. H. Llewellyn. They later shared many Las Cruces experiences.

Branigan moved to Las Cruces in 1886 where he soon began farming and raising horses in partnership with Llewellyn. On the farm they developed and maintained a vineyard and orchard and specialized in producing wine and honey. Both of the partners soon joined the Las Cruces unit of the Territorial Militia. In 1897 Branigan married Alice Montgomery, a local teacher and accomplished musician. He later served terms as county assessor, school board member and city commissioner and then was postmaster as an appointee of both Presidents Teddy Roosevelt and William Howard Taft.

Thomas Branigan died in 1925 and in 1932 his widow, Alice, willed the family home and other property to the City of Las Cruces. A subsequent 1935 gift provided the city with thirty-five thousand dollars for a library building (Branigan Memorial) and furnishings and ten thousand dollars for books. She also granted the city another ten thousand dollars for a youth recreation center. The library building which Mrs. Branigan's bequest funded now houses the Branigan Cultural Center.

William Henry Harrison Llewellyn was born and educated in Wisconsin and Iowa. He spent eight years seeking his fortune in the gold mines of Montana with only limited success. From 1881 - 1885, he was Indian Agent for the Mescalero Apaches, then moved to Las Cruces and opened a law practice, joining the firm of

Las Cruces Post Office, 1912. Postmaster Capt. Thomas Branigan in cap, Mrs. Branigan in bonnet.

Rynerson and Wade. In 1886 he married Ohioan I. M. Little, a marriage which produced seven children.

Llewellyn served under Teddy Roosevelt in the Spanish American War, was named Captain of Troop G, and after meritorious service at the battle of San Juan Hill, was promoted to Major. He was appointed to terms as U. S. Attorney, District Attorney and District Court Judge and served as Speaker of the New Mexico House of Representatives. When he was appointed Judge Advocate General of the New Mexico National Guard, he was promoted to the rank of Colonel. He also was an outspoken advocate of statehood for New Mexico.

Mrs. C. B. (Josephine) Smith's grandparents, the Sotos, emigrated from Mexico to the Mesilla Valley in 1886. Within eight years Don Jose Maria Soto had been appointed Justice of the Peace. All ten of their children were educated at the Presbyterian Mission School (current site of Central Elementary School). Their son-in-law, Ricardo Triviz, daughter Zenaida's husband) was one of only two sheriff candidates to successfully challenge the Lucero brothers' thirty-six year domination of that office in the post-Pat Garrett era. Josephine's mother, Leva, was the only Hispanic in Las Cruces High School's sixteen-member 1915 graduating class. Leva married Alberto Gutierrez and together they built a home and apartments on San Pedro Street near the Soto home. Josephine was their only child.

C. B. Smith's father and grandfather worked for years for American Smelting and Refining Company (ASARCO) facilities in northern Mexico. Both were killed in 1917 by Pancho Villa's forces. That forced C. B.'s mother, Luisa Sauceda Smith, to load her mother and five children into a box car and cross the border to El Paso, then on to Tortugas, just south of Las Cruces. C. B. and three of his four siblings graduated not only from Las Cruces High School but from New Mexico A. & M.

After holding a teaching and basketball coaching job in Mesilla, C. B. Smith turned to what proved to be his lifelong work and love, home building. He started with adobe structures, buying single lots, and the completion of each house provided funds to buy the next lot. He was completing five or six houses a year. By the 1960s, however, he organized a modified assembly line approach and completed fifty to fifty-five homes a year. C.B. recalled that his last land purchase came when the seller complained that he had twenty acres which he would never be able to sell because they were located in an arroyo. C. B. offered him $350 for the entire twenty acres, took possession and turned the area into the very successful Arroyo Plaza shopping center on East Lohman.

C. B. and Josephine were married in El Calvario Methodist Church, which C. B. had built. Josephine Smith was the first Hispanic lady elected to the Las Cruces Board of Education. All of their five children

Las Cruces Post Office, 1912.

graduated from Las Cruces High School and three also earned college degrees, two from New Mexico A. & M. and one from University of New Mexico. Their son, Ruben, served in the New Mexico House of Representatives for nine years and was the first elected mayor of Las Cruces, now serving his seventh year.

E. J. (Jeno) Stern was born on a small farm in Hungary in 1885. His mother hoped he would be a rabbi, his father urged medical training and Jeno aspired to be an engineer. So in 1903 he packed his bags and violin and headed for the United States. He spoke no English and upon arrival at Ellis Island, immigration officials renamed him Eugene. He worked for an immigration agency in New York for a year, moved on to Houston, then to El Paso. He went to work on meat delivery wagons and after six years became a supervisor. He then began traveling in a one horse buckboard peddling meat to places like Vado and the Dripping Springs Hotel.

By 1910, Gene moved to Colorado to sell insurance. While there, he met and in 1913 married Mable Armes Lull Nye, a shy Nebraska girl who lived with a foster family because her mother had died in child birth. The Sterns soon moved back to New Mexico and homesteaded 160 acres south of Las Vegas. Gene continued to sell insurance and sewing machines, but built a one bedroom frame house, a well, windmill and a check dam on the arroyo.

In 1915, Gene became a naturalized citizen but declining sales led them to move to Las Cruces. Their first home was an Amador Hotel room. Gene worked at his uncle's Boston Store on South Main until he could negotiate purchase of his own mercantile site. Late in 1918, he leased what had been known as the Jacoby Store at Las Cruces and Main and renamed it Stern

Mercantile. By 1920, he was able to buy a building next to his Stern Store, established the Popular Dry Goods, and in 1923 bought another adjacent building to expand the Popular.

Meanwhile, Gene and Mable had built their first real home on North Miranda for what became a family of six children. In 1926 .he sold the Popular to the Rosens and built at 221 North Main what he named the White House, to be managed by Bob McMillan. In addition to nearly thirty years in merchandising, Gene became a partner in Mutual Building and Loan, helped revitalize the First National Bank after the depression-related bank holiday, and founded State Finance Company. Gene bought the old Park Hotel property to the north of Pioneer Park in 1939 and had a new two-story home built on that site.

Not only was Gene a prime mover in building Las Cruces' Temple Beth El but he also generously supported Catholic causes and St. James Episcopal Church, and paid off a $60,000 outstanding debt of the Boys (and Girls) Club. He reportedly contributed a half million dollars to construction of the Scottish Rite Cathedral. In drought years he loaned money to farmers at low interest rates. Mable was a life member of the Women's Improvement Association and the Progress Club., active in the Order of Eastern Star and started the local chapter of the Order of Rainbow for girls.

Aside from his many charitable contributions, possibly the most memorable community gift of Gene and Mable Stern was the matched pair of bronze lions which grace what then was the new City Hall on North Church Street. Twenty years earlier the Sterns had admired the work of Mexican sculptor Barios Caballero in Mexico City. In 1968, Gene commissioned Caballero to cast a matched pair of magnificent beasts, male and female, for

$25,000. They were formally dedicated in August, 1968.

One of Las Cruces most widely known post-World War II professionals has been astronomer Clyde Tombaugh. It was he who, as a young high school graduate employee at Lowell Observatory in Flagstaff, Arizona, discovered the planet Pluto. As a result of that discovery, he received a four-year scholarship to Kansas University, where he met and married Patsy Edson, the sister of one of his astronomy classmates.

Clyde depended on his 1930 black Model T Ford to enable him to alternate work at Lowell Observatory and completion of bachelor's and master's degrees at Kansas University. In the war years, 1941 to 1945, Clyde joined the permanent staff at Lowell and also taught navigation to Navy officer candidates at Northern Arizona University in Flagstaff. After a year as an astronomy professor at UCLA, Clyde was recruited by Patsy's brother to come to White Sands Proving Ground (later known as White Sands Missile Range) near Las Cruces. Clyde's assignment was to supervise rocket photography as Chief of Optical Measurements. The Tombaugh's first

The Park Hotel, just north of City (Pioneer Park).

home in Las Cruces was the El Molino Motel on the future site of the First National Bank Tower.

After ten years at the Proving Ground/Missile Range, Clyde received a grant to research small natural satellites to explore possible hazards to rockets entering outer space. To secure funding for the research, which was to be conducted at the equator, Clyde moved to a research adjunct facility at New Mexico State University, the Physical Science Laboratory, and also to an NMSU faculty position. He taught at the University from 1955 until retirement in 1973. Not only was he actively involved throughout that period in developing a highly respected Department of Astronomy at the university but after retirement, he established a Tombaugh Endowment to finance astronomy scholarships and professorships. To support the endowment, he and Patsy then undertook fund raising speaking tours which took them to nineteen states, fifty-three cities and three Canadian provinces

Patsy and Clyde were charter members and co-founders of the Unitarian Universalist Church of Las Cruces and were active in development of the church's present sanctuary on South Solano Drive. Memorial stained glass windows honoring Clyde Tombaugh are in production by Jackie Clark and will soon be installed in that sanctuary.

The earliest agriculture researcher in the Las Cruces area definitely was Fabian Garcia. He was born in Chihuahua in 1871 and was reared by a grandmother. He moved to Las Cruces at the age of fourteen, and was taken into the home of Thomas Casad. He became a United States citizen in 1889, and was among the earliest students admitted in 1890 to the new College of Agriculture. Encouraged by Hiram Hadley, he mastered English and completed his Bachelor of Science degree in four years, with an intense interest in entomology and agricultural pest control. He was a member of the College's first graduating class.

By 1895, Fabian was named meteorologist and assistant in Horticulture at the Experiment Station and by 1899 was promoted to the rank of Assistant Professor. He quickly won further promotions, as Station Horticulturist and Department Head in 1901. He completed graduate work and a Master's degree at Cornell University and ultimately became Director of the A. & M. Experiment Station in 1923. Fabian devoted a lifetime to successful research and publications in both Spanish and English on horticulture and farm insect control. He was awarded honorary doctoral degrees from both the University of New Mexico and New Mexico A. & M.

Possibly the best known, most respected agricultural scientist in New Mexico history and a worthy heir to the Fabian Garcia legacy was Roy Nakayama, also known as "Mr. Chile." Roy's father, Kaichiro Nakayama, was born into a family which had harvested rice in Japan for 1,200 years. He migrated to the United States in 1908. Taking the name John, he toured the west but settled in Nebraska, farming in partnership with a German immigrant.

Injured when thrown from a horse, John decided to look for more healthful, temperate climes and headed southwest, stopping in El Paso. He learned that fertile land was available in the Mesilla Valley and that some Japanese immigrants already lived there. The family then moved to the Las Cruces area, renting farm land which had belonged to the Shalam Colony. Son Roy was born in 1923 in what had been the Children's House at Shalam.

The 1910 census revealed only two persons of

ᴥ Successful Families ᴥ

Japanese descent living in the Valley. Both were males and worked as cooks, one in the home of Percy Barker and the other employed by Oscar Lohman. However, between 1910 and 1920, there was a significant influx of Oriental residents, possibly because of the publicity given to completion of Elephant Butte Dam and its promise of extensive irrigation. The 1920 census reported thirteen Japanese-American households, totalling thirty-three people, twenty-seven of them adults, all of them employed in agriculture.

New Mexico's 1918 alien land law and the Oriental Exclusion Act forbade land ownership by "persons ineligible for citizenship" (and all foreign-born Orientals thus were by law ineligible to own land). That meant these non-citizen residents had to overcome significant personal, social and legal obstacles in order to become owners rather than renters of land. Consequently, when by the mid-1920s John Nakayama had saved sufficient funds to buy his own farm, it had to be in the name of Roy's twelve year old brother, Carl, who by virtue of having been born in this country (Nebraska), was a U. S. citizen. It was arranged that Pat Campbell, then of Mesilla Valley Bank, would hold the land in trust until Carl's twenty-first birthday.

Roy entered Las Cruces High in 1937, the fifth Nakayama to do so. He graduated in 1941 with an excellent academic record and very active participation in Future Farmers of America. He completed two years at New Mexico A. & M., but then volunteered for service in World War II. Called to active duty in May, 1943, he was assigned to the 159th Infantry, was sent to Europe and in December, 1944, was captured by the Germans during the Battle of the Bulge. Several months as a prisoner of war left him so weakened that upon returning to civilian life, he knew he was not physically capable of full time farming but also knew he wanted an agriculture-related career.

During the war, the Las Cruces area experienced much the same anti-Japanese agitation as did most of the country. Not only had local newspapers begun to headline the "Japanese problem," but in 1943 and again in 1945 nearly one thousand Valley land owners signed a pledge not to sell land to Japanese-Americans. A Doña Ana County Anti-Jap Association formed to try to stop all Japanese immigration. Consequently, when Roy Nakayama returned to the Las Cruces campus as a decorated veteran, it was to learn that New Mexico A. & M. refused him admission "because he was Japanese." Fortunately, his pre-war professors spoke out, insisting upon his admission. Once graduated, he paid his way through master and doctoral programs at Iowa State. After interim employment with the California Department of Agriculture, he became an Associate Professor in 1960 at New Mexico A. & M.

Roy specialized in plant pathology and plant breeding, conducting extensive research in both pecan and chile development. Chile was, however, his great love and chile and Roy soon became inseparable. It was said that the innovative spirit, curiosity, patience, persistence and attention to detail that developed *Big Jim*, *R Naky* and *Espanola Improved* were present in every thing that Roy Nakayama did. He never stopped trying to improve his pecans and chiles and, incidentally, his golf. Working with students, he was thorough and demanding, yet respected and loved. Upon his retirement in 1988, one colleague said Roy was the best researcher he'd ever known and the best horticulturist the college ever had. One college administrator estimated that by the time of his retirement, Roy's work was contributing more than ten million dollars annually to New Mexico's economy.

✿ Successful Families ✿

When Roy's older brother, Carl, graduated from New Mexico A. & M. in 1937, he had reached the age of twenty-one. That meant the original farm purchased in his name in 1928 was signed over to him. Carl, Roy and their father then bought an additional one hundred acres. Another Japanese family, the Yabumotos, had lived in California for some years but moved to Chamberino and bought a twenty-five acre farm south of Las Cruces in 1915. In 1940, Toshi Yabumoto and Carl Nakayama were married. While Roy was devoting his professional career to agricultural research, Carl and Toshi and their three daughters were making practical application of research results in developing a highly successful Nakayama farming operation.

Contrary to the impression left by the preceding pages of this chapter, women as well as men were making significant contributions to the Las Cruces area. Included should be Calla K. Eylar Wolfe. She was Doña Ana County School Superintendent from 1932 to 1934. She then served five terms in the New Mexico House of Representatives from 1940 to 1950, at that time only the second Doña Ana woman in history to be elected to the legislature. She was House Majority Floor Whip in 1943-44, only the second woman in history to hold that position. A graduate of Michigan State University, she and her husband had come to El Paso in 1914. He was an El Paso County judge and lawyer and she was supervisor of home economics in the El Paso public schools from 1923 to 1926. The Eylars moved to La Mesa in 1915. Their daughter is Mrs. Hershel (Anne) Zohn.

At least two women have made major contributions to Las Cruces' Branigan libraries. One of the earliest local librarians was Mrs. M. M. (Sara) Swartz. She served on the Branigan library board for more than a quarter century, part of it as vice-chairman, and was memorialized for her long service on that board by the naming of the east children's room at the original Branigan building the Sara Swartz room.

Helen Caffey was born in the Philippines and received her college-level library training at the University of Colorado and Emory University. Her librarian employment began in Atlanta and then in California, but in 1950 she joined the staff at Branigan, where she served for more than twenty years. Helen was the Doña Ana County Historical Society's Hall of Fame honoree in 1970 and retired in 1971.

Katherine Doughty (Katie) Stoes was born in Minnesota, made a trip to New Mexico by covered wagon, but was educated in Minnesota. She was the wife of merchant Henry Stoes and is remembered as one of the Valley's largely self-taught but most skilled historical writers. She taught courses at New Mexico A. & M., served on the College's Board of Regents, was active in the Women's Improvement Association and even drove the club's dust-settling water wagon. She also served several terms as Doña County School Superintendent, was chosen New Mexico A. & M. Woman of Achievement in 1957 and named to the Doña Ana County Historical Society's 1962 Hall of Fame.

Elizabeth Fountain Armendariz was the recipient of Doña Ana County Historical Society's very first Hall of Fame award in recognition of her development of the Gadsden Museum and in opening it to the public in 1931. Elizabeth was the granddaughter of Albert Jennings and Mariana Perez Fountain and the museum features many memorabilia from the Fountain career and family.

Mrs. Clara Belle Drisdale Williams is remembered for her remarkable academic accomplishments, her talented children and her longevity. Her record at New

✿ Successful Families ✿

Mexico A. & M. provides evidence the College had quietly begun student admission desegregation as much as twenty years before the city's public schools. She had been quietly enrolling in summer sessions beginning in 1934 and is believed to have been the College's first black graduate, with a bachelor's degree in English awarded in 1937. She was permitted to enroll in the graduate school in 1939 and her son, Charles Lee Williams was admitted in 1941.

An honorary doctoral degree was awarded to her by the university in 1980 and a campus street was named in her honor. A Clara B. Williams endowed scholarship to NMSU was established in her name in 1991. She taught for twenty-seven years in the Las Cruces school system and was elected to the National Education Association's New Mexico Hall of Fame. Her three sons, James, Charles and Jasper all are NMSU alumni and medical doctors. Clara Belle died in 1994 at the age of 108. She always reminded her children and her students of her credo: "Get your education and make something of yourselves and don't let anyone tell you you can't do it."

Another family which deserves to be recognized in any history of the area is the Fielder family. Gertrude Hibler Fielder, daughter of Daniel and Ollie Hibler, was believed to be the first black child born in Las Cruces. The Hiblers had moved to Las Cruces from Texas so Daniel could work as chef at the Don Bernardo Hotel. In the mid-1920s, there was no high school for black children, so Gertrude eventually earned her G. E. D. diploma and completed two years of training at NMSU. She was bilingual both in reading and writing and in the 1960s, Las Cruces schools hired her as an aide in the Head Start program at Washington School. She had taught earlier at Phillips Chapel CME Church which at one time was used as an elementary school for black children. The church, built by Gertrude's father, was the oldest black church in Las Cruces.

Her son, Clarence, began teaching in Las Cruces schools in 1949, earned his bachelor's degree at NMSU in 1950 and his Master's degree in 1955. He saw combat service in the Korean War, winning the Purple Heart and Silver Star for gallantry in action. He returned to teaching in 1952 and continued that career until 1983. Clarence was named Teacher of the Year in 1970. For twenty-eight years he has been teaching a Black History course at NMSU. In 1996 he was appointed to the Las Cruces School Board and currently serves as the Board's president.

This volume has made occasional references to the question of public school segregation and, after 1955, desegregation. One female educator who should be recognized because of her involvement in the desegregation process is Mary Swisher. She had been an African-American teacher in segregated years, teaching black students. When the decision was made to desegregate local schools, she was terminated. She appealed her dismissal to the superintendent, the local School Board, the State School Board and the District Court. At each of these levels, her appeal was denied. When she appealed the case to the State Supreme Court, her dismissal was rescinded and she returned to her former teaching position.

George Adlai Feather was born in Iowa and because of his parent's health, moved to Artesia, New Mexico ,in 1906. He earned bachelor's and master's degrees at University of New Mexico, then saw Marine Corps duty in World War I. He then studied in England under a Rhodes Scholarship and earned a degree from Oxford University. He came to the Mesilla Valley at the age of thirty-one in 1923 and taught languages at New Mexico

A. & M. He even served as an assistant football coach in the 1926 season. Although proficient in fourteen languages, Adlai left teaching in 1935, turned to farming and opened a nursery, which he sold in 1952 to Lewis Emerick. As a long time student of New Mexico history, he then set out to visit and study the records of every community, past and present, in New Mexico. He also was an active and dedicated supporter of the Sister of the Good Shepherd and their schools.

Another much loved and respected public school teacher of the mid-20th century was Edith Berrier. She was born in Iowa but came to the Valley as a child and attended school at Mesilla Park, graduating from high school at the old Central School on Alameda. She taught in Missouri and then at Alamogordo, but returned to teach in Las Cruces in 1934. She taught at Mesilla Park, Fairacres and Mesilla elementary schools for a total of thirty-four years. Edith earned a Master's degree at NMSU and did further graduate work at Columbia and University of Southern California.

She was president of Doña Ana Teachers Association and a life member of both New Mexico Education Association and Delta Kappa Gamma. She retired in 1972.

Chapter 10
⊛ The Proving Ground ⊛

The decade of the 1930s, between the Depression and World War II, was a period of much progress for Las Cruces. While it was not yet a large city or a boom town, the population of Las Cruces more than doubled, from 3,969 in 1920 to 8,385 in 1940. Another fifty percent population gain occurred in the next decade, rising to 12,325 by 1950 (See Appendix #3). Local media reported in 1939 that as many as 150 new homes had been built since the post-depression bank re-opening. For much of the 1930s, Sam Klein was mayor (See Appendix # 2). During his tenure as mayor, twenty blocks of streets had been paved, a new storm sewer system had been completed and a new pueblo style city hall had been opened. A $70,000 Branigan Library structure had opened and $4,800 per year was promised for new book purchases. Las Cruces Union High School had added a new home making cottage and Superintendent of Schools C. S. Conlee had announced plans for a new $77,000 Court Junior High School. In the business community, Anthony's Dry Goods had opened on the Main Street site of the Don Bernardo Hotel. Three airports were operating rather informally, one at New Mexico A. and M. A., another at Hanger Lake on the east mesa, and a third, called Crawford Field, on North Solano.

There still were, however a few reminders of the "good old days." In 1937 two men, Henry Lorenz and Harry Dwyer, unsuccessfully attempted to rob the Southern Pacific's Apache Limited as it headed west from El Paso. Unfortunately one train employee was killed in the struggle to overpower the two "modern Jesse Jameses", both of whom took up residence in the Santa Fe State Prison. "Get rich quick" schemes still popped up, also, as it was in 1937 that Milton "Doc" Noss reported finding gold and religious articles at Victorio Peak, an alleged treasure trove still unrecovered.

Even though 1,345 banks had closed and humorist Will Rogers described the early 1930s as "no money, no banks, no work, no nothing," the depression did not seem to have as marked an effect on Las Crucens as it did in other areas. Certainly Las Crucens were acutely aware of the streams of dust bowl and depression refugees headed for California, who passed through town and headed out West Picacho Avenue. In fact, they began to refer to West Picacho as "Little Oklahoma."

When local banks reopened, they moved into cotton, financing cotton brokers and accepting cotton as security. Although an estimated fifteen million people were unemployed at the depths of the depression, New Deal emergency relief programs did help. The Works

Progress and Public Works Administrations (WPA and PWA) began to provide relief both to individuals, who worked for $18.75 a week, and for community infrastructure needs. Included in the 116,000 buildings worked on nationwide by these people were improvements at Elephant Butte Dam, construction of three local schools, including Court Junior High, the Doña Ana County Court House, Kent Hall on the A. and M. campus, the Visitor's Center at White Sands National Monument and even the Tom Lea mural at what now is Branigan Cultural Center. Several Civilian Conservation Corps (CCC) camps also were located in the area, including one at what is now the El Paso Irrigation District office on Melendres and another at the old Walmart site on Lohman. There also was a camp in the Ft. Selden-Radium Springs area. These young men worked on numerous conservation, flood control and tourism/recreation type projects.

World War II quickly affected many aspects of Las Cruces life. Nearly 2,000 New Mexicans were war prisoners or internees of the Japanese in that war. About 1,400 of the state's National Guardsmen had been activated as the 200th Coast Artillery Corps as of Jan. 1, 1941, nearly a year before the Japanese attack on Pearl Harbor. They trained at Fort Bliss (which soon had more than 25,000 men in training). During the war, many men also trained at Alamogordo and Deming Army Air Bases and at a Navy bombing range west of Las Cruces.

Once in the Philippines, members of the 200th were the first to fire on the enemy and the last still fighting at the time of the Corregidor surrender. Gen. Jonathan Wainwright called the 200th "the finest fighting unit in the Philippines." Many of them died on the Bataan Death March or suffered torture and malnutrition in the

Women's Improvement Assn. Parade Float, 1944.

prison work camps. They suffered a forty-seven percent casualty rate. Of those imprisoned by the Japanese, twenty-three were from the Las Cruces area. In the Philippine theater of operations, fatalities included ten Las Crucens, three from Mesilla Park, two from Doña Ana and one from Mesilla (See Appendix #8).

Of the 2,263 New Mexicans who died in World War II, 124 were former New Mexico A. & M. students. All told, more than 2,000 ex-Aggies had served in the military, 549 of them as commissioned officers. In the first month of the war, the College gained its first "hero". Lt. William C. "Bill" Porter, a former Aggie, was acclaimed as a "second Sgt. York" for single-handedly "picking off" a nest of Japanese soldiers in Luzon.

New Mexico A. & M. enrollment of course dwindled. Total enrollment in 1940 was 935 and by 1943, it was down to 209 (See Appendix #4). However, men in the Army Specialized Training Program (ASTP), arriving in groups of 500, and the 750 men in Navy training programs eased the overall effect on the campus.

Another consequence of the war was the shortage of farm labor, which led to establishment of an Emergency

Farm Labor Program,. This involved use of prisoners of war, with the exception of Japanese. There were Prisoner of War (POW) base camps at Lordsburg, Roswell and Santa Fe but branch camps were located near the sites of greatest farm labor shortages, particularly cotton growing areas. Thus, branch camps were at Las Cruces, Hatch, Deming and Anthony. For housing, former CCC barracks and other abandoned buildings were pressed into service. More than 900 prisoners were supervised by county extension agents and were considered welcome additions to the strained labor pool. Farmers in the Las Cruces area later reported the Germans were very good workers, but not so the Italians. The prisoners received prevailing wage for the work but all but seventy five cents a day was held in trust for them until the war ended.

Las Crucens joined world wide 1945 celebrations of war's end, with VE (Victory in Europe) and VJ (Victory in Japan) days marked by community-wide festivities. Among returning veterans were four Medal of Honor winners, Alexander Berryman, Jr., John C. Morgan, Alejandro R. Renteria and Robert S. Scott. Veterans returned to shortages of housing and consumer goods but many took advantage of G. I. Bill opportunities to open higher education access to a professional future. The first two veterans to return to campus were Philip "Shorty" Heick from Hagerman and Clarence Chase from Ruidoso.

Builders like Dale Bellamah, Jamie Stull and the aforementioned C. B. Smith soon were remedying the housing shortage with accelerated productivity. Relative prosperity returned and the city was ready for another celebration in 1949, its centennial. Under the chairmanship of Mayor Sam Klein, a board of directors was selected to plan the commemoration. Directors were

August 30, 1953. Flood on west Picacho Avenue.

future mayor Tommy Graham, Jess Lydick, Seaborn
Collins, A. C. Wright, E. F. Adams and Luis Maynez.
That board decided to prepare an elaborate pageant,
entitled "La Gran Fiesta" to be presented on seven con-
secutive nights at the New Mexico A. & M. football stadium. Because southern New Mexico autumns are usually the most temperate, pleasant, lovely seasons of the
year, October 9th to 15th dates were selected. The
Centennial Committee raised $150,000 by selling stock
in the event, enabling them to hire a Hollywood company to design sets and costumes. Twenty-nine Valley
beauties competed to reign as Fiesta Queen and the performance involved thirty-five horsemen and more than a
thousand participants.

The week opened with Centennial services in most
churches. The Fiesta's opening performance was preceded by a parade and the crowning of Queen Teresa
Viramontes. The dramatic extravaganza consisted of sixteen episodes plus a prologue and a finale. Episodes
included "The Legendary Years," "Flags Over Mesilla."
"Tortugas and the Virgin of Guadalupe, "Dear Old
Golden Rule Days," "The Pioneer Women of the West,"

and "Lest We Forget." Proving once again the old adage
regarding "best laid plans," two hours before the opening
night curtain was to rise, a beautiful October evening
was struck by a violent windstorm, scattering tents,
props and costumes. Undaunted, organizers regrouped
and rebuilt and by the next night were ready to present
the entire Fiesta as scheduled. The celebration was
judged a great success.

The Las Cruces area probably has suffered no more
and no less frequent much-publicized but unsolved murders in its background than other similar cities. One
such crime, possibly second only to the Fountain disap-
pearances in notoriety, occurred in 1949. On Easter
Sunday, a nineteen year old Deluxe Cafe waitress, Ovida
"Cricket" Coogler, disappeared. Seventeen days later, her
body was located in a shallow grave, with evidence that
cause of death may have been that she was run over by a
vehicle. A former Aggie football player, Jerry Nuzum,
and a black World War II veteran, Wesley Byrd, were
arrested. Although Byrd had been seen at the Deluxe
Cafe, he was never formally charged, and the case
against Nuzum was dismissed, even though he had been
with Coogler earlier in the evening.

After more than 300 citizens signed petitions
demanding it, a grand jury investigation uncovered widespread illegal gambling and bribery to protect gambling
interests. Lodges, veterans' halls, clubs and casinos were
raided, huge piles of slot and other gambling machines
were burned at the court house, and indictments for
gambling and alcohol violations were returned against
fifty-two persons. While not implicated in the Coogler
murder, which rumor suggested was accidental, Sheriff
A. L. "Happy" Apodaca and two of his deputies were
tried on charges of ignoring widespread gambling and of
violating the civil rights of Coogler case suspect Wesley

Byrd, who it was alleged had been tortured while incarcerated. The sheriff was not convicted on gambling-related charges but he and his deputies served ten months in prison on the torture civil rights offenses. No one ever was convicted of the Coogler murder.

Scarcely five years after the end of World War II, the country found itself involved in another armed conflict, waged thousands of miles from the continental United States. President Truman led the nation in a successful "police action" to prevent Communist forces from overrunning the entire Korean peninsula. A number of Las Cruces young men, some of them World War II veterans, were called upon to serve their country from 1950 to 1953. By the time an armistice was signed in July, 1953, after thirty-seven months of fighting and $18 billion dollars of U. S. expenditures, South Korea's independence had been preserved but more than 50,000 American lives had been lost and 100,000 more had suffered serious injuries. North Korean conquest of the entire Korean peninsula had been thwarted and the danger of another world war with China and even Russia had been averted.

The next major boost to the economy and growth of Las Cruces came as a delayed consequence of the rocket research of Robert H. Goddard. It should be noted, however, that two Goddards, unrelated, born within five years of each other and reared in the same area of Massachusetts impacted on New Mexico. Ralph Willis Goddard, born in 1887, grew up in Worcester, Massachusetts and in 1911 earned a Bachelor of Science degree at Worcester Polytechnic Institute. By 1914, he was head of the Electrical Engineering Division of New Mexico A. & M. School of Engineering and in 1920 was named Dean of Engineering at the College. Always interested in wireless telegraphy, Ralph Willis Goddard established and developed a 10,000 watt campus radio station, KOB. Unfortunately, Ralph was fatally electrocuted in 1929 while adjusting station equipment. The station ultimately was sold to NBC and relocated in Albuquerque.

The "other" Goddard, Robert Hutchings Goddard, was born in 1882 and he also earned a Bachelor of Science degree from Worcester Polytechnic. His graduate study led to Master and Ph. D. degrees at Clark University. The Massachusetts scientist patented a vacuum oscillator tube as early as 1920. Financially supported by Charles Lindbergh and the Guggenheim foundation, he devoted the next decade to research in rocket flight and patenting of multi-stage rockets. Both because he suffered from tuberculosis and because New Mexico was an ideal setting for rocket testing, Goddard maintained his base of operation in the Roswell area from 1930 to 1941. In effect, he changed military artillery and bombing emphasis from a gun powder base to gasoline. However, United States military leaders were slow to realize the potential of rocketry, even as Germany's V-2s rained destruction on England Even until his death in 1945 Goddard insisted the Germans had stolen his engineering secrets to develop their deadly rockets.

As early as 1938, however, War Department officers came to New Mexico seeking an extensive isolated, desolate, level region for a long-range artillery firing range. Col. Hugh Milton met with them and suggested the Tularosa Basin, stressing its moderate climate, nearly unlimited visibility and sparse population. The Army agreed and, after the bombing of Pearl Harbor, accelerated the process of purchases, leases and condemnations of hundreds of square miles, roughly the size of the state of Connecticut. In addition to the clear skies and flat terrain, the military liked the fact that the Basin was not crossed by rail or air lanes and was surrounded by hills and mountain foothills which provided good observation points for optical instruments.

Meanwhile scientists had been engaged in highly secret research into the feasibility of nuclear weaponry at a remote Los Alamos laboratory in northern New Mexico. Those scientists selected a barren area which they called Trinity Site at the northern end of the Tularosa Basin to test their new weapon. The success of the July, 1945, test led to the dropping of two nuclear bombs on Japan and, in turn, ended World War II.

The Alamogordo Bombing Range had been established early in the war and crews of some of the U. S.'s heaviest bombers had trained there. By February 8, 1945, the Army Corps of Engineers declared the land proposed for White Sands Proving Ground to be an area of military necessity. Then, addition of portions of Ft. Bliss Artillery Range and all of the Alamogordo Bombing Range was approved later that month. By that time the Ordnance Department of the Army finally had begun to develop working models of rockets and guided missiles. They contracted with California Institute of Technology to conduct missiles research and the first U.S.-developed rocket test firings took place at California's Edwards Air Base in 1945.

On June 12, 1945, with war against Japan predicted to continue for some months, Congress appropriated money to develop what initially was named White Sands Proving Ground. It then was divided into north and south areas. The north area, east of White Sands National Monument and north of Highway 70, was controlled by the Army Air Force and included the Alamogordo Army Air Base and the Alamogordo Bombing Range, about forty by one hundred miles in size. The south area was adjacent to the Fort Bliss

Target Range and was about forty by twenty miles in area. They later were combined, except that Alamogordo's Army Air Base went through a red tape process of being deactivated and then reactivated as Holloman Air Base early in 1946.

As it became evident in early 1945 that the war in Europe was winding down, Dr. Wernher Von Braun's team of German scientists, who had developed the V-2 rocket at Peenemunde, opted to surrender to the U. S. Army. By July, 1945, the Army had seized rocket parts and designs. Von Braun and 450 colleagues were moved to Bavaria, then a select contingent was secretly moved to the United States in what first was called Operation Overcast, and later Operation Paperclip, based on the fact that paper clips were placed on the personnel files of those selected.

The German designs and equipment were moved to Las Cruces by 300 railroad cars and then by caravans of flat bed trucks to the chosen site east of the Organ Mountains. Initial plans were for the site to be strictly a test facility with no housing on base, so the Germans were housed at Ft. Bliss and transported daily to the Proving Ground. The only paved road from El Paso was via Las Cruces, although the more direct unpaved Old Salt Trail (War Road) was available, except when it rained. The basis of the missile program was to be the resurrected work of Robert Goddard and the unprecedented technological advances the Germans had made.

Transmission power lines were strung from Elephant Butte to Las Cruces to White Sands. Administrative and work buildings were razed at Sandia Air Base in Albuquerque, transported to the Proving Ground and rebuilt. On July 9, 1945, one week before the Trinity site atomic test, formal dedication of the Proving Ground occurred. Within a month, 163 anti-aircraft personnel

arrived from Ft. Bliss and by late November 370 personnel were stationed in "hutments" or pyramidal tents.
Barrack construction began in early 1946, and by late
that year the base boasted seventy-four buildings.
Although these included old CCC buildings and barracks transported from what had become Holloman Air
Base and other sites, the shift to permanent facilities was
under way.

That shift was accelerated after a January, 1947,
storm blew 4,000 square feet of roof off the V-2 assembly
building. Also, by July, 1946, 350 civilian personnel
were added, The Army appropriated $400,000 for civil-
ian housing, and a post surgeon was appointed. In the
first two years, military facility needs alone resulted in
$8.5 million in construction. Early in development of the
site, the move to unify U. S. military branches under the
Department of Defense also was implemented at White
Sands. By October, 1945, Navy personnel were assigned
and Army Ordnance soon after offered the Navy a test
site. In June, 1946, a Naval Ordnance Unit was formally
established.

A total of sixty-seven V-2 rockets were assembled
and tested, not entirely without mishap. In May of 1947,
one V-2 went off course and crashed northeast of
Alamogordo. Two weeks later, a mis-connected gyro-
scope caused a V-2 to head south rather than north and
land in a cemetery in Juarez. Instead of disrupting a
fiesta going on nearby, Juarez entrepreneurs roped off
the crater and charged admission. White Sands officials
are justifiably proud of the fact, however, that for more
than fifty years the range has not been responsible for a
single public (non-employee) injury.

By 1947, about 200 Germans were quartered at
Officers Barracks on base while several dozen more
were still at Ft. Bliss. American civilian engineers had

begun to replace their German counterparts, many of
whom opted to remain in the Southwest. General Von
Braun was later named director of the U. S. Army's
Ballistic Missile Program. Of course, Las Crucens soon
were finding employment at the base and local firms
were beneficiaries of much of this development. For
instance, Hayner and Burn Construction Company won
the contract to build the first missile launching platform.

By 1950, Las Cruces had grown to a population of
over 12,000. Gov. John Dempsey recognized the growth
and officially designated it as a "city." Initially, long time
residents of Las Cruces were apprehensive over the
influx of German scientists, the fear of V-2 rockets landing haphazardly over the area and the number of military personnel in evidence. In fact, one of the early Base
Commanders, Col. Harold Turner, threatened to place
Las Cruces off limits to military personnel unless and
until soldiers were "treated as human beings."

From that point on, community relations did
improve. Las Cruces service clubs such as the Elks Club
hosted good will banquets and dinner dances and special
events honoring post officials. Post commander Philip
Blackmore invited public groups to attend firings and
insisted that Las Cruces and El Paso were the post's
"closest associates." Proving Ground personnel partici-
pated in Las Cruces' 1949 Centennial celebration and in
Armed Forces Day and campus Homecoming parades.
Las Cruces contractors were urged to speed home building projects. In the early stages of Proving Ground
development, close relationships also were established
with the University's Physical Science Laboratory.

As early as 1946, New Mexico A. & M. Physics professor George W. Gardiner and as many as twenty-five
faculty members and graduate assistants began guided
missile research in an old Aeronautics Building on cam-

pus. By Fall semester of that year, Professors George
and Anna Gardiner announced formal creation of the
Physical Science Laboratory (PSL). Their first projects
resulted from a contract with White Sands Proving
Ground to perform computational work, supplemented
by New Mexico state funds.

College-Missile Range cooperation snowballed. From
soon after the Proving Ground's opening, A. & M. faculty began to teach some classes on post. For other
courses, the Range provided transportation to campus
and paid up to seventy-five percent of tuition. By 1954,
there were eleven classrooms at the Range, and as many
as 1,500 men were working toward G. E. D.s, or vocational specialization, or undergraduate and even graduate degrees. A. & M. President John W. Branson and
the post commander, Brigadier General George G. Eddy,
in 1952 organized cooperative programs involving six
months work at the Range and six months academic
work on campus, with a degree possible after five years.

Winston Churchill's famous Westminster College
speech warning about the "Iron Curtain" signalled a

Las Cruces City Hall.

chilling of relations between World War II allies and the
onset of the "Cold War." By September, 1948, the
Proving Ground became a permanent base and major
defense firms became sub-contractors. The first contract
was with General Electric but Douglas, Western
Electric, Glenn Martin Company, Bell Laboratories and
Johns Hopkins Applied Physics Laboratory soon followed. When the Department of Defense designated Las
Cruces a critical housing area, builders announced plans
for 200 new homes.

With the outbreak of war in Korea, with its fear of
Russian and/or Chinese Communist involvement, activity at the Proving Ground was further accelerated. In
1952 the V-2 program was terminated but the Secretary
of Defense designated the Base an integrated missile
range, shifting 158,000 acres of Fort Bliss land to the
range. Sections of land at the northern extension of the
range also were added on an "as needed" basis, meaning
ranchers located in those areas would occasionally be
asked to temporarily move to town at government
expense while test rockets were fired in the direction of
their land. Missile firings increased from 86 in 1951 to
1,198 in 1955 and construction funding jumped from
$400,000 in 1949 to $4.1 million in 1954. By 1955, the
base had 3,200 civilian employees and 3,400 military personnel. In 1958, the Proving Ground was renamed
White Sands Missile Range.

Russia's launch of its Sputnik space vehicle in 1957
shifted much of the U. S. scientific emphasis to what
some termed a space race. President John F. Kennedy
announced this nation's determination to place a man on
the moon. New Mexico's Gov. Edward Mechem asked
Frank Papen to head a delegation to meet with the
President in 1962. Their goal was to champion the
Missile Range's potential for space-related Project

◎ The Proving Ground ◎

Mercury and the proposed Projects Gemini and Apollo preparation. While the actual meeting with the President was cancelled at the last minute, the Papen group was able to successfully advocate the Range's readiness to analyze booster engines and systems, and to test rockets and rocket recovery. Soon thereafter, the Range expanded to the west side of the mountains and the National Aeronautic and Space Administration (NASA) opened its space-related Lyndon B. Johnson test facility. By 1992, White Sands Missile Range was Doña Ana County's major industry, employing nearly 10,000 people.

Subsequent budget balancing and Department of Defense funding cuts reduced the size of the Missile Range work force to 7,000 in 1997 and, in 1998, to approximately 6,700, counting civilian, military, contractor and NASA operations; Nearly half are civilian employees, ten percent are military with that portion of the work force decreasing. The balance are contractor employees. At least fifty percent of employees live in Las Cruces. The Range's 3,200 square miles mean it still is, area-wise, the largest military installation in the country and the Department of Defense's only all-overland test range. In 1997, the Range spent $433 million in the local area.

Chapter 11
❧ Renewal ❧

With major impetus provided by the G. I. Bill, post-war New Mexico A. and M. enrollment steadily grew. For example, in 1946, the 1400 member student body included 900 veterans. The emerging technological revolution and evolution of the space age were placing ever-greater demand on trained engineers, technicians and computer specialists. Higher education was compelled to gear up to meet the challenge. Dr. Roger B. Corbett had assumed the presidency of New Mexico A. and M. in 1955. He was an agricultural economist, with a Ph. D. from Cornell University. He had been employed by the American Farm Bureau and the U.S. Department of Agriculture, and when he accepted the A. & M. presidency, was an executive in the National Association of Food Chains in Washington, D. C.

❦ Renewal ❦

By 1956, the new president was ready to institute changes in the nearly seventy year old, 2,600 student institution. He announced his "Big Plan" to enhance the breadth and quality of education offered. His first two steps were necessarily related, although they took two years to implement. First, he initiated the steps necessary to significantly expand graduate programs. Secondly, he then felt it appropriate in 1957 to call for an institutional name change to New Mexico State University. In 1958, although there were regent and alumni protests, that change was approved. During the Corbett administration, many new buildings were added, the Ph.D. programs were initiated, and research cooperation with White Sands Missile Range was strengthened. He also took a strong stand to keep the university functioning in a period of national and campus student unrest. His fifteen year tenure set a length-of-service record for NMSU.

As mentioned earlier in this volume, McFie Hall, a two story fourteen room building, was the only campus building for several years. It burned to the ground in 1910, but a new administration building, to be called Hadley Hall, had opened in 1909. The Seed House, built prior to 1892, is the oldest building on campus. The Science Hall, built in 1896, was the second major construction project and was razed in 1974, after more than three quarters of a century of use. However, the YMCA building, Trost designed, is located next to the present Music Recital Hall and is the second oldest remaining building, having been built in 1907. It currently is the subject of a fund raising drive by the University's Cornerstone Campaign for Excellence, designed to preserve and renovate it.

Although the University is situated on a 5,000 acre campus, early growth of the physical plant had been

slow and somewhat disjointed. However, architect
Henry C. Trost did develop a campus plan in the period
after World War I. The engineering building, designed
by the Trost firm and built in 1913, was named Goddard
Hall in memory of former Engineering Dean Ralph
Willis Goddard. In the mid-1930s an annex was added
with WPA help. Another renovation of Goddard Hall
presently is under way. Young Hall, named for Judge R.
L. Young, was built in 1928 as a library but housed the
English Department from 1958 to 1982 and then became
the home of Military Science and Aerospace Studies.

After three decades with no official residence for the
college president, the regents proposed in 1917 that a
presidential home be built "in a style befitting a president
of a growing university" at an estimated cost of $8,000.
Designed by the Trost firm and built facing north on
University Avenue by Bascom-French Company of Las
Cruces, the total price proved to be $9,560. In 1966, a
one story addition was built. In the summer of 1980,
however, a new presidential residence was completed on
Geothermal Road, overlooking the University Golf
Course.

Enrollment had plummeted during World War II,
with the 1945 graduating class totalling only nineteen.
However, enrollment effects of the G. I. Bill soon made
it necessary to depend upon trailers, quonsets and barracks to handle students desiring on-campus student residences. The G.I. Bill bulge also created a markedly
increased need for part-time student employment. For
more than fifty years, the George Gardiner-founded
Physical Science laboratory has provided employment
not only to many local professionals but also to hundreds
or even thousands of students on co-operative and part
time work arrangements. It also has played a major role
in NMSU's becoming a highly regarded research univer-

sity, and it should be noted that the present on-campus Physics Building was named for Dr. Gardiner.

In the 1950s buildings such as the Branson Library, Hamiel Residence Hall and, in 1957, the Memorial Tower to honor those who had perished in World War II were added. The 1960s and 1970s have been termed the growth decades for the University. President Corbett, with the assistance and experience of Academic Vice President Bill O'Donnell, should be credited with initiating the pattern of physical plant growth, which is evident on today's campus.

Dr. Corbett's successor, Dr. Gerald Thomas, sustained that growth momentum in his 1970 to 1984 tenure. A new Student Activity Center, and a Student Union building named for Dr. Corbett were completed in 1970 and both underwent major remodeling and additions in 1997. The Pan American Center, a $3 million 12,000-seat basketball and concert facility, opened in late 1968, is informally referred to as "the house that Lou (Coach Henson) built." That project and the 31,000 seat football stadium completed in 1978 were, from the perspective of construction difficulty, the major building accomplishments of these decades. In the 1980s the English-Speech, Business and Music Complexes were added.

As the University celebrated its centennial in 1988, enrollment at the Alamogordo, Grants, Carlsbad and Doña Ana branch colleges and the main campus totalled 18,000. By Fall, 1997, that total was over 23,000. The average student age was twenty-five and they represented all fifty states and, with the increasing enrollment of foreign students, eighty countries. Seventy percent were receiving some form of financial aid. The University's current research contracts at that time totalled $70 million.

Included in the University's service functions are
twelve agricultural and livestock research centers and
thirty-three county extension offices. Two of the state's
Research Centers of Technical Excellence, established by
the Rio Grande Research Corridor, are located at
NMSU; the Plant Genetic Engineering Lab and the
Computing Research Lab. Evening classes and the
Weekend College are especially helpful to students holding full time jobs but desiring additional education. Doña
Ana Branch College, located in the southwest quadrant
of the campus, has for twenty-five years, relieved the
main campus of responsibility for offering technical,
vocational, remedial and pre-professional courses. It now
enrolls more than four thousand students.

Currently, in addition to 900 professional staff and
1200 classified staff, the University's main campus has
670 full time faculty, eighty percent of whom hold
earned doctoral degrees. It currently is ranked by the
Carnegie Foundation for the Advancement of Teaching
as a Level I research institution, one of the eighty-eight
top research universities in the nation. Its two libraries
hold nearly one million volumes and seven thousand different periodicals. The university has six undergraduate
colleges, seventy-five different disciplines, fifty areas of
Master's level study and twenty Doctoral level programs.
The most recent statistical analysis reports that the more
than six thousand college and Doña Ana Branch
employees hired directly by NMSU constitute more than
25% of the county's work force, pay $573,000 annually
in property taxes and $8.1 million for utilities. The
University is the county's second largest employer.

After World War II, Las Cruces' Main Street underwent an evolution which was to significantly alter the
nature of that street and the city itself, but stir contro-
versy from that day to this. Actually, what happened to

◈ Renewal ◈

Las Cruces' business district conformed to a pattern which was affecting small to medium size cities all over the country. Main Street had been the business, social and religious hub of the city, even to the Saturday night phenomenon of teen age drivers by the hundreds "cruising Main."

The chain reaction was triggered by the abandonment and then demolition of historic buildings at the south end of the city's business district. First, Loretto Academy was abandoned and razed and Main Street straightened to extend south. The Academy was replaced by the First National Bank and Tower and, in 1965, Loretto Mall, the city's first air-conditioned, enclosed shopping center. As the new mall prospered, a parallel pattern of what seemed irreversible abandonment and deterioration struck the Main Street business district.

It was at about this time in the mid-1960s that a program called Urban Renewal was proposed as the cure-all solution to the problems of Main Streets all over the country. It was the culmination of a series of federal initiatives which began with the Housing Act of 1949, and expanded with 1954 and 1959 revisions of the Act. With the stated goal of city rehabilitation, the federal government agreed to provide two-thirds of the land acquisition, relocation, and administrative costs.

City leaders viewed urban renewal as an excellent opportunity to revive the historic downtown area. An exploratory committee, chaired by Main Street businessman Rex Ross, studied the city's options and in 1965 submitted an Urban Renewal plan, which promised to create a modern, vibrant, heart of the city in the area surrounding Main Street. An Urban Renewal Agency was established and Earl Whelpley was selected as executive director.

Nine million dollars were spent on the seven block

down town mall and surrounding area, $6,750,000 of it federal funds and the rest from the city. Basic tasks of remodeling or demolition and relocation began in July, 1968. By mid-1973, demolition of an entire neighborhood in the original town site district had relocated eighty-four families and fifty-two individuals. With the basic relocation grant of $5,000 per family, only eight families bought, at least initially, and two-thirds rented. Operators of more than 160 businesses in the renewal area had a choice of remodeling or relocating. Only thirty-eight remodeled, at a cost of nearly $700,000, while approximately 100 relocated. The balance just ceased operation. By 1974, Main Street had become a pedestrian mall, with a winding yellow brick walkway shaded by metal awnings. Local construction firms certainly profited from the program.

Predictably, however, the urban renewal program was not universally popular with affected residents and business persons. Although not actually a phase of or financed by Urban Renewal, possibly the least popular of all the projects undertaken in that time period was demolition of St. Genevieve's Church. As mentioned earlier, the deteriorating condition of the church building made preservation and restoration seem to Catholic diocesan officials impractical. Monsignor William Ryan, who at that time served Las Cruces churches, recalls that unsafe conditions had caused the state of New Mexico to condemn portions of the building. He recalled that stop gap measures such as shortening of the two towers, building buttresses against the outside walls and installing tie rods were proving inadequate, largely because the original building had such insufficient and deteriorating foundations. To many Las Crucens, however, urban renewal and St. Genevieve's demolition will always be inseparably related and criticized. The comment still often heard is that "the architectural heart of the city" was destroyed. There also were complaints that residential remodeling or demolition regulations discriminated against ethnic Hispanic residents.

Although a local newspaper called the program "the most important local event of the decade," the downtown area has not prospered. It has become an area of offices, service providers and empty buildings but not the promised vibrant heart of the city. Popular Dry Goods and Coas Book Store remain, but probably no more than a dozen retail outlets continue in business. One interesting development opened, however, at the same time as the Downtown Mall. It was expected to serve as a prototype for future mall projects. La Esquina, an eight tenant building designed by Gerald Lundeen and built by C. B. Smith Company is in space once occupied for years by the Schenk Bakery. Businesses continue to occupy the building. but few similar projects have developed.

In recent years, much discussion has centered on possible upgrades or modifications of the mall. Parking and building access, especially rear entrance access, have been improved. One portion has seen experimental replacement of the metal awnings with landscaping, with evaluation of long-term results yet to come. Conversion of the original Branigan Library and adjoining building to an art gallery, historical museum, sculpture garden and cultural center and the placing of historic-oriented bronze sculptures and plaques on the mall have improved the appearance and potential of the area.

Proposals now are being heard regarding placing a convention and performing arts center at the north end of the mall. In fact, the sesqui-centennial committee planning the six-month celebration has earmarked any funds remaining after the event to serve as seed money toward a convention center-performance hall project. Coupled with Branigan Cultural Center, this certainly would revitalize the north anchor of the mall and it is hoped would attract tourism-related hotels and restaurants. Elmo Baca, a specialist in renovation of urban downtowns, recently challenged civic leaders to develop "a shared artistic and business plan for revitalization of our downtown."

The most successful use of the downtown area has been the Farmer's and Craft Market, which since 1971 has set up on Wednesday and Saturday mornings to offer a wide variety of home grown agricultural and homemade craft products for sale. Over two hundred vendors sell their wares and produce each Wednesday and Saturday. It has become a local shopping and social gathering place and a popular tourism attraction.

In 1980 the Mesilla Valley Mall, located a mile east of downtown and easily accessible from Interstate 25, opened. Dillard's, Penney's, Sears, Service Merchandise, and Beall's have served as retail anchors ever since. The mall opening triggered a major shift of business and traffic focus. The Lohman-Telshor-Interstate 25 area has become the retail center of Las Cruces. However, as mentioned earlier, the old Loretto Mall, attractively renovated and modernized, now is named Loretto Towne Center and not only houses federal, state and professional offices, but also is headquarters for the Citizens Bank and Las Cruces Public Schools. Only one space has remained a retail outlet, Anthony's Department Store. It recently became Beall's, but has been for years a sort of south anchor to the old downtown, occupying the space which once was Luby's Cafeteria.

Concurrent with and as a natural consequence of economic, industrial and population development of Las Cruces, facilities providing medical care were begun

soon after the turn of the century and continue to prosper and expand. General practice physicians came and
went, beginning even before the Civil War. For instance,
physician and surgeon Dr. J. A. Butler opened practice
in 1861. As mentioned earlier in this volume, in the post-
Civil War period, the first hospital facilities were established to provide care for tuberculosis victims.

In the early 1890s, Col. Eugene Van Patten homesteaded in the Dripping Springs area of the Organ
Mountains, twenty miles east of Las Cruces. Over the
years he developed a resort. Early in the 20th Century,
New Mexico college students and townspeople made
many excursions "out to Old Van Patten's." By 1897 the
Dripping Springs facility included a building described
as a "hotel for tuberculars" and was, in fact, the first
tuberculosis sanatorium in southern New Mexico.
Financially over-extended, Colonel Van Patten sold the
property in 1917 to Dr. Nathan Boyd. Boyd had worked
early in his life as a physician on a cruise ship. While so
employed, he met and married his wife in Australia.
When she developed tuberculosis, he decided to settle in
the Mesilla Valley and bought the Dripping Springs
property in the hope that it would prove a therapeutic
site for his wife. He soon announced plans to build a
larger sanatorium at the Springs but they never material-
ized, as his medical practice gave way to a career
described earlier in this volume as land speculator, real-
tor, banker, promoter and even an aspiring Rio Grande
dam builder. Later he bought much of the old Shalam
Colony property, talking again of sanatorium plans, but
accepted therapies for tuberculosis were changing and
those plans were abandoned.

Dr. Robert Edwin McBride, a Louisianan who, like
Boyd, was motivated to move to the southwest's semi-
desert by his wife's respiratory problems, arrived in the

Mesilla Valley in 1904. He soon established not only a medical practice but also a tuberculosis sanatorium, consisting of a two-story building and a row of tents in the Townsend Terrace area on the north side of Las Cruces. His first house, at 1905 Alameda, and his medical facility were for years referred to as "the Alameda." At that time he and a Doctor Donaldson were the physicians serving "the Alameda".

The "rest and fresh air" approach to tuberculosis therapy soon was replaced by drug treatment and sanatoriums were closed or converted to other uses. Dr. McBride had by then established a very successful local practice and was active in civic affairs. He not only served terms as president of the New Mexico Medical Society and as editor of its journal but from 1917 -1921 served as Doña Ana County School Superintendent.

In 1935, Dr. McBride started the town's first community hospital in a former residence at Water and Hadley streets. It was intended as a temporary facility to lessen local dependence on El Paso until a Las Cruces hospital could be built. Dr. Leland Evans provided equipment for

"The Alameda" Sanatorium (early 1900s).

what initially was a three bed facility. An adjacent home soon was acquired and the hospital expanded to twenty-five beds, with a maternity ward and provisions for minor surgery. It soon boasted a staff including Drs. Evans and McBride, James and William Sedgwick, A. D. Maddox and L. L. Daviet. Dr. McBride retired from active practice in 1939.

More than ten years later, Mayor Samuel Klein led a campaign to build Las Cruces' first full-service community hospital. The federal Hill-Burton program provided $250,000 and construction at the site on South Alameda, near its junction with South Main, began in 1949. Awaiting actual opening of the facility, medical supplies and equipment were purchased but had to be stored in a barn on the Branigan property. The hospital informally opened on Apr. 13, 1950. By May of that year Memorial General Hospital was operating as what then was considered a full service eighty-four bed medical facility. In 1966, a 2,000 square foot $75,000 emergency room annex was added and an intensive care unit soon also was added.

By 1965, however, community growth had made Memorial General inadequate for rapidly developing space, equipment and technological needs and preliminary discussions had begun on expansion or relocation options. In 1971, a new building, constructed by Frank Tatsch builders, rose on South Telshor Boulevard, near University Avenue. The fifty-acre site was leased from New Mexico State University. Jointly owned by Doña Ana County and the city of Las Cruces, the 160 bed hospital opened in 1971 and in 1982 added two floors to bring capacity to 286 beds. The former hospital, on Alameda, now serves as a city government office building.

In 1990, with its name changed to Memorial Medical

Center, it has become a full service, fully accredited facility with steadily expanding staff and available services. Since 1990, additions have included the cardiovascular diagnostic laboratory; the mobile lithotripsy kidney treatment unit; the Ikard Memorial Cancer Treatment Center; and the coronary surgical unit for open heart and angioplasty surgery. Also added have been the ambulatory care center, specializing in endoscopy and ambulatory surgery; a renovated maternal/infant care unit; and a Promptcare unit. The center also has acquired the capability for MRI, ultra sound, CAT scanning, mammography, and EKG and stress testing.

Memorial Medical Center certainly has achieved impressive statistical records. In 1997, they recorded nearly 15,000 in-patient stays, more than 2,600 births, 38,000 emergency department visits, 354,000 laboratory procedures, and 4,000 skilled nursing care days. One very significant current statistic is that in 1997, the Center provided over $19 million in non-reimbursed indigent services. With more than 200 physicians available, 1,300 employees, and 150 active volunteers, the Center in 1997 paid $47 million in wages, benefits and taxes and spent $2,710,000 with local businesses.

In 1998, a major change in management structure was approved. The name was changed to Memorial Medical Center, Incorporated, referred to as MMC, Inc. The physical plant's fifty-acre site still is owned by Las Cruces and Doña Ana County, but operation and management are the responsibility of MMC, Inc. It still is a not-for-profit operation but the new arrangement lifts some of the restrictions and regulations which made it difficult to deal with reduced federal and state funding. The new arrangement also enables MMC, Inc. to compete and/or cooperate more effectively with managed care and for-profit entities. Terms of the lease require

continued providing of indigent care, and rent is to be
paid on a regular basis to New Mexico State University,
Las Cruces and Doña Ana County. Change of name and
management structure have not changed the makeup of
the administrative team. Steve Smith continues as president and Chief Executive Officer. Current directors are
physicians Catherine Kemmer and Vital Pai and Bruce
Streett, Mick Gutierrez, James Bullock and Nancy
Arnold.

On May 30, 1998, President Smith and the Directors
announced plans for an eleven million dollar, 40,000
square foot MMC, Inc. Health-Plex to be located in
northeast Las Cruces, with construction to begin in summer, 1998. When it opens in twelve to eighteen months,
the Health-Plex will house facilities for outpatient
surgery and endoscopy and expanded laboratories.
Correlated with the new northeast facility's construction,
major remodeling will commence, in the fall of 1998, on
the main MMC campus. This will provide a new
women's services center, including obstetrics and gyne-
cology departments. This will in turn free up space to
begin converting semi-private rooms to private ones.

It should be noted, however, that Las Cruces also has
an additional hospital, the eighty-six bed Mesilla Valley
Hospital on North Del Rey Boulevard .There also are at
least four clinics, Family Medical, La Clinica De Familia,
Lovelace and the recently opened Veterans
Administration Clinic on Don Roser. The state also has
recently moved its Public Health Offices into newly
remodeled quarters on North Solano.

Increasing numbers of senior citizens are opting to
make Las Cruces their retirement home. One of the
consequences is a mushrooming of home health care
businesses. In mid-1998 fifteen Las Cruces concerns
offered home health services. In addition, Mesilla Valley

Hospice has served Las Cruces since 1982 and now has moved into newly remodeled quarters on East Montana Avenue, including an eight suite hospice house designed to offer inpatient services. Hospice now has nearly thirty employees and relies heavily on 135 volunteers.

Chapter 12
❧ Fabulous Future ❧

New Mexico's official motto, adopted long ago and seldom repeated, but as relevant as ever is *Crescit Eundo*, meaning "It Grows As It Goes." New Mexico and Las Cruces are growing and will continue to grow, but continued growth must be termed a mixed blessing. With every boost in population, additional demands are placed on the services and infra-structure of the community. The City of the Crosses was in 1997 the seventh fastest growing metropolitan area in the United States. From 1990 to 1996, the region grew nearly 20%. Census statistics project that New Mexico's population will continue to increase by nearly two percent per year at least until 2025, making the state second only to Hawaii in expected rate of growth. Factors such as creation of new jobs, high birth rate, lovely scenery and climate, proximity to the Mexican border, and the effect of the North American Free Trade Agreement all explain the optimistic projections.

Las Cruces now is the state's second largest city and is projected to grow at an annual 2.2% rate, which would produce a population approaching 80,000 by the year 2000. A number of inter-related factors contribute to this optimism and the city's growth potential. Included are the proposed free trade zones and the increased traffic at the new Santa Teresa port of entry. There also are plans in the international border area for an extensive inter-modal transportation facility, which already have resulted in extensive border area highway construction and improvements at the Las Cruces International Airport. Industrial parks, such as the one on Las Cruces' west mesa, are proliferating and expanding.

Although it is far from assured, the possibility also exists of development of a major spaceport in the desert area northeast of the city, either on or just north of Missile Range property. Sites in seventeen states are being publicized as optimal potential spaceport locales, but the north section of the Tularosa Basin site and in the Oro Grande area South of Alamogordo still are in the running. Suggestions also have been heard that the White Sands Missile Range might be converted, at least in part, to a spaceport facility. Advocates recall the space shuttle landing in that area in 1982 and also cite recent preliminary testing of potential re-usable space vehicles at the Range and at Holloman Air Base. While it is not directly relevant to the possibility of a local spaceport, residents of a far northeast suburb of Las Cruces recently voted to incorporate as Spaceport City making it potentially New Mexico's 102nd city. The fact that only sixty-two citizens voted and that those sixty-two represented seventy-eight percent of the eligible voters provides something of a reality check, but on the other hand, Spaceport City may prove to be the community with a future.

Economically, it must be acknowledged that both New Mexico and Las Cruces have suffered somewhat, compared to the rest of the Southwest. Unemployment figures have tended to be higher than in neighboring states, although it is estimated that the various levels of government-federal, state, county and city-employ 19,500 people, thirty per cent of the county's total.

The area also actively woos industries seeking to relocate near the border. A state agency, the New Mexico Border Authority, and a public-private agency, the Mesilla Valley Economic Development Alliance are charged with publicizing the potential of the area. The city also has two active chambers of commerce, the Greater Las Cruces Chamber, directed by Joe Biedron, with nearly 800 members, and since 1990-1991, the 400 member and growing Hispaño Chamber, directed by Arnulfo "Nufie" Hernandez. Both home and commercial construction figures continue high. In May, 1998, contracts for future construction totalled nearly five and a half million dollars and for the first five months of 1998 totalled nearly forty-three million dollars.

The fact that a national magazine recently ranked Las Cruces the tenth most livable small city in the west suggests that city government is coping well with its growth. It was officially designated as a city in 1946, with a city-manager form of government. It now is governed by six councilors elected from districts and a mayor who, since 1991, is elected at large. They in turn hire a city manager, currently Jesus Nava. City government attempts to take a proactive rather than a reactive stance toward Las Cruces' unique urban problems. Innovations, at least for this area, have included police bicycle patrols, neighborhood policing, and a new set of programs called the "neighborhood revitalization effort." City councilors and staff are scheduling regular "listening sessions" in their neighborhoods to receive citizen input, to which they attempt to actively respond. The goal is to head off potential problems and attempt to solve those already existent.

An inevitable consequence of growth in any nation committed as is ours to education of its young has been development of extensive educational facilities. A century ago, the aforementioned South Ward School, at what now is the corner of Alameda and Amador, was the city's only public school, after having served as the first site of Las Cruces College. C. W. Ward was at that time serving as the school's principal. The original South Ward building closed in 1926, was demolished and was replaced by a new building. When the new South Ward School was partially destroyed by fire, the building was refurbished in 1935 as the Las Cruces Public School administration building. That building, in turn, was vacated in 1991 when administration offices moved to the remodeled Loretto Towne Center site. The vacated building shortly thereafter was destroyed by fire.

As to the historical background of school administration, in 1904, Isidoro Armijo chaired a newly elected school board, comprised of Capt.Thomas Branigan and Jose Gonzales. It organized Doña Ana County School District #2, naming W. O. Evans as principal, at $80 per month, and hiring five teachers and three janitors. Within a year they had engaged the Trost architectural firm to design Central School for a fee of $286.50. Within a few years, the brick building, constructed at 150 North Alameda Avenue, became the community's first high school. In 1925, when the Union High School was built a few blocks north at Alameda and Picacho,

❖ Fabulous Future ❖

Central's original brick building was demolished and replaced by an adobe structure which still serves to this day as Central Elementary School.

In those early years, two policy decisions troubled educators and ethnic groups. For some years, not only was there no sort of bilingual education but speaking Spanish was prohibited, even on the play grounds. Secondly, the schools shifted from a racially integrated student body which existed in the first thirty years of public education to segregating black students in the mid-1920s. In 1926 black students were sent to Phillips Chapel School, at the corner of Tornillo and Lucero. In 1934 , a four room adobe school was built at Chestnut and Solano, referred to originally as "the colored school," and in 1938 re-named Booker T. Washington School. At times, the school served elementary, junior high and high school students. In addition, as mentioned earlier, there was a time when even Gadsden School District was bussing its black students, mostly residents of Vado, to Washington School. However, by 1954-55 , with the consolidation of the Las Cruces Municipal Schools with the six remaining Doña Ana County schools, all Las Cruces schools were fully integrated.

In 1927, Holy Cross Catholic school was built, large-ly by donated labor and materials and by assorted fund raisers. By 1941, Court Junior High was built on the site of the first county court house with W. P. A. labor. In 1956, Las Cruces High School opened at El Paseo and Boutz. In less than a decade, in 1965, Mayfield High School opened on north Valley Drive and in 1993, Oñate High School opened on far northeast Main Street.

At present, Superintendent Jesse Gonzales oversees twenty-one elementary schools with another in the plan-ning stage, seven mid-high and four high schools. These schools serve a combined enrollment of over 22,000 students, more than 2,800 employees and an annual budget of more than $150,000,000. There also are at least three private schools, Immaculate Heart of Mary, Holy Cross, and Mesilla Valley Christian.

The Las Cruces Public School System also owns the building which formerly housed Court Junior High and now is the Court Youth Center. After more than ten years in development, the Center now offers after-school, weekend and summer arts, physical and sports activities for children aged three to seventeen. The Youth Center staff has expanded its programming to include a Safe After School program, every school day afternoon at Washington School, and a Thursday afternoon program for fourth and fifth grade girls at MacArthur School. For pre-schoolers, a program for developmentally disabled four year olds has been initiated. In addition to these, a "building skills for employment" program is available for teens.

The development of Las Cruces' park system was somewhat analogous to the fact that Las Cruces survived for decades with either no public school or, near the end of the nineteenth century, only the South Ward School. Similarly the early years had only improvised parks until, thanks to the Women's Improvement Association, Pioneer (City) Park was developed. However, in recent years, the city has done an excellent job of developing parks, museums, galleries, and tourist attractions.

The city now has fifty-seven parks, eighteen public tennis courts, and three golf courses, with another eighteen-hole course and a twenty-four hour driving range under construction on its eastern fringes. It has thirty-acre Burn Lake for swimming and fishing, three public swimming pools plus private pools at the University and at the city's two country clubs. Not only does the city attempt to provide recreation facilities for its residents, but those residents illustrate a do-it-yourself philosophy when it appears necessary. When voters failed to approve plans for a taxpayer funded, covered, year-round swimming pool and a skate board park, citizens combined volunteer labor and contributions to cover and update Frenger Pool and to develop a skate board facility near Meerscheidt Recreation Center's BMX biking track. There also is evidence of city determination to include attractive landscaping and mini-parks in its main thoroughfare improvement projects such as Missouri-Boutz, Spruce-Picacho and Triviz.

Meerscheidt Recreation Center is an extensive, well-equipped facility, including a number of baseball, softball and soccer fields. As to indoor activities, it includes indoor gyms, table games, a weight room, racquetball and basketball courts, a roller hockey rink and year-round scheduled classes in activities such as aerobics, dance, gymnastics, physical conditioning and self defense. A recent addition to the city's recreation menu is Club Fusion, in Mesilla Park, a teen club offering a full snack bar, video games, a pool table, parties and dances in a safe, non-alcoholic environment

The city also maintains varied activity schedules at Casa Arriba, Mesilla Park, Henry Benavides, Robert Munson and East Mesa Centers. They cater especially to senior citizens, although the Mesilla Park and Benavides facilities feature not only morning and early afternoon hours for senior citizens but additional hours for all ages. Munson Center is the largest facility, a multi-purpose Senior Center open to all citizens over age fifty. In addition to a wide variety of recreational and educational services, most of the centers also serve lunches. For instance, Munson Center serves about 250 lunches per day. Another senior center, Hospitality House on North Alameda, although not a city-sponsored facility, also offers senior-oriented programming..

Activities and services have in fact remarkably proliferated in the last decade. The Southwest Area Agency
on Aging coordinates many of the activities. In one
recent year, the Meals on Wheels program delivered
670,000 meals. The Road Runner Transit system, Dial-a-
Ride and Safe-ride services are especially helpful to
senior citizens. University Terrace Good Samaritan
Village, located on a sixteen acre site east of Telshor and
offering a variety of accommodations for those over age
sixty-two, is the oldest of the city's centers for retirement
living. Founded in 1979 under the leadership of retired
NMSU faculty member Ralph Stucky, and expanded in
1996-97, its accommodations include 253 units for independent, assisted living or medical circumstances.

Recently opened is the Cottonbloom Adult Living
Center on the north side. Opening in Fall, 1998, on
Roadrunner near North Main, will be another retirement complex, to be called the Village at Northrise. Its
173,500 square feet of buildings will feature units for
independent living, for assisted living, and for those who
experience dementia. Designed for residents aged fifty-
five or older, it also will feature an underground parking
garage. In addition there are nine nursing homes available in the city.

Other educational and cultural opportunities for
senior residents have been offered in recent years. The
Academy for Learning in Retirement offers informative
and entertaining programs, usually arranged in four half-
day sessions, and often including luncheon arrangements. New Mexico State University also offers courses
especially designed to cater to seniors, including the
Community Education program at the Doña Ana
Branch. University faculty also offer a number of self-
improvement courses at Munson Senior Center

⚜ Fabulous Future ⚜

Museums and galleries have tended to multiply and prosper in recent years. Museums include the Museum of Natural History at Mesilla Valley Mall; the University Museum at Kent Hall on campus; and the Space Murals Museum and White Sands Museum and Missile Park east of the city. Also open to the public are the Law Enforcement (Sheriff's) Museum, the private Gadsden Museum, founded in 1931 and featuring Fountain family memorabilia, and the Log Cabin Museum.

The latter museum is a pre-1900 structure, of hand hewn logs, transported from the ghost town of Grafton, New Mexico, in the Gila's Black Range. It was donated by Mr. and Mrs. Sid Blakely as a part of the nation's 1976 bicentennial celebration. Mr. and Mrs. Myron George led the campaign to finance the dis-assembling and re-assembling of the structure and the Las Cruces Home Builders Auxiliary furnished the cabin with 19th century memorabilia. The Museum is located at the north end of the downtown mall in what is called the Bicentennial Park.

After construction of the present Branigan Memorial Library in 1979, the city dedicated the vacated library building on the Downtown Mall to development of the Branigan Cultural Center, which opened in 1981. The building just south of the Center also was purchased in 1991 and the Cultural Center soon will include two museums, the Las Cruces History Museum and the Museum of Fine Arts, separated by a memorial sculpture garden and a patio paved with memorial bricks.

The city also has other sites awaiting development for which it encourages public input. As mentioned earlier, the Downtown Mall is administered by the Parks and Recreation Department and has hosted the Farmers and Crafts Market for twenty-seven years. However, the city and its citizens are dissatisfied with the present status of

the mall, believing that it could become a true civic center as well as the site of the Market. The city is actively
soliciting suggestions as to the mall's future. Las Cruces
also purchased in 1992, and since has partially renovated, the eighty-eight year old Santa Fe Depot building
and has recently purchased the Women's Improvement
Association building adjacent to Pioneer Park. City ownership should ensure preservation of the buildings but it
is to be hoped that they will not have to stand unoccupied or unused.

The newest jewel in Las Cruces' museum offerings,
although it is state-owned and operated, is the New
Mexico Farm and Ranch Heritage Museum, located on a
forty-seven acre site on East University Avenue near "A"
Mountain. Although still being developed and planning a
formal opening in October, 1998, the museum now is
open to the public. Dr. William P. Stephens, former
director of the New Mexico Department of Agriculture,
and former New Mexico State University President
Gerald Thomas spearheaded the evolution of plans and
fund raising which led to construction of the 70,000
square foot building. Both men, well aware that agriculture, beginning with the hunters and gatherers of prehis-
tory, made New Mexico possible, formally stated the
museum's mission as "So the Future May Know -To
honor those who have kept the faith and the land in protection."

When completed, the Farm and Ranch Heritage
Museum will include a permanent gallery with 20,000
square feet of exhibits and a temporary gallery with
changing displays and exhibits. It also is to feature an
indoor theater and outdoor amphitheater. The public
will be invited to view a working dairy barn and black-
smith shop, live farm animals, an antique farm equipment exhibit and demonstration working farm and ranch

fields. Also operating soon will be a gift shop, restaurant and farmer's market,

Exhibits in the Heritage Museum emphasize the vital role of water, controlled and effectively distributed, to the future of agriculture as well as the cities of the Valley. The reason this is and should be emphasized is that in 1980, El Paso sued New Mexico, seeking access to ground water within New Mexico. The 1906 treaty drawn up in preparation for damming the Rio Grande at Elephant Butte obligated New Mexico to provide El Paso with an annual allotment of water. As the combined population of El Paso and Juarez approached one million, the Texas city proposed to drill wells at two sites north of the Texas-New Mexico border. El Paso's water needs were due not only to growing population but to the fact that what is called the Hueco Bolson of underground water, running under El Paso-Juarez, is drying up at an alarming rate. Las Cruces' water advantage is that southern New Mexico's Mesilla Bolson is constantly being replenished by irrigation water seeping back into the underground supply. Another concern of area farmers, especially those in the El Paso-Juarez valley, has long been and still is that of controlling the salinity and impurity of the river's water.

After eleven years of animosity and litigation and a court ruling overturning New Mexico's water exportation ban, new water laws were written and both sides settled on creating a water commission to mediate the disputes. Hydrological studies are ongoing, which will determine the nature and number of water treatment plants needed. El Paso already has several such plants and research may indicate the need for further plant construction at Las Cruces and Juarez. At this point El Paso's plea is for a constant flow of Rio Grande water year round, rather than seasonally reduced flow because of New Mexico's farming irrigation needs. Studies and discussion continue, also, as to who legally owns the water- the cities? the farmers? the states? the federal government? Elephant Butte Irrigation District? Final resolution of water problems awaits research results and may be several years away.

Especially in the last two decades, tourism has become a major industry in and around Las Cruces. The city's Convention and Tourism office and its Chambers of Commerce work diligently to publicize the City of the Crosses and its many scenic, artistic, cultural and historic attractions. In its pre-automobile decades, Las Cruces was noted for its downtown hotels, often providing horse-drawn transportation to and from the Santa Fe depot. Today, however, the city boasts thirty-three motel-hotels, seven bed and breakfast facilities, and seven residential areas specifically for manufactured homes.

The City of the Crosses has become an increasingly popular center for art and artists. A few decades ago, artists such as Juliet Amador, Aileen Shannon, Marjorie Tietjens, Hester Roach, Dorothea Patterson Weiss and, at the College, Ken Barrick and Paul Mannen were considered a sort of "pioneering art colony." Today, however, the city offers twenty-five different art galleries, including those at the Mesilla Valley Mall, Branigan Library and Cultural Center and the University, as well as a number of private galleries.

One unique expression of the city's love of both its history and its art is the number of folk art murals gracing water tanks in and around Las Cruces. Travelers and locals are fascinated by and pause to admire a total of eleven colorful tanks in the area--five in Las Cruces, three in Truth or Consequences and three in Silver City.

Three tanks within Las Cruces plus the three in Truth or Consequences were painted by local artist Tony

Pennock, starting more than twenty-five years ago. The two east of town were painted by former local resident Royce Vann. The murals feature such events as Oñate's *entrada* (entrance) into New Mexico, Columbus' discovery of the New World, the vital role of water to New Mexico's agricultural development, space exploration, and early day mining and transportation. Folk art murals also adorn walls at scattered locations such as Branigan Memorial Library, Klein Park and throughout the city.

Las Crucens love to discuss other uniquely local folk art features which have become popular, or at least hot topics of discussion. They include a huge roadrunner created from a multiplicity of types of "junk" by local artist Olin Calk. The "Big Bird" greeted visitors to the east mesa land fill for several years but now is being renovated while a new permanent nesting site is located. Another distinctive artistic feature, requiring a very loose definition of art, is the Sound Off column in the city's one daily newspaper, the Sun News. It offers an opportunity for any caller to anonymously record his opinions and hope the paper's editors will select that observation as one of ten or so which are published daily. Another long term art-related discussion topic is the yellow "mushroom" sculpture at the entrance to the Harold Runnels Federal Building. Still another more recent "art" object is the grove of colorful man-made, waterless palm trees on Boutz Avenue.

There are other manifestations of the interest which has developed in recent years in the culture and history of the area. The Doña Ana County Museum Society was formed in 1939. In the late 1950s Harry Bailey wanted to give the land on which Fort Selden stood to the state to be designated as a state monument. To facilitate the Ft. Selden transfer and to conform to existing tax laws, the Doña Ana County Museum Society incorporated in

1961 as the Doña Ana County Historical Society. Louis Freudenthal, Betty Bowen and G. Adlai Feather signed the articles of incorporation. Freudenthal and Feather served as the Society's first two presidents. Another step toward historical preservation came in 1971 when Dr. Monroe Billington and NMSU President Gerald Thomas founded the Rio Grande Historical Collections, to be housed in NMSU archives and managed by archivist Austin Hoover. It has become a treasure trove of artifacts, photos, documents and personal memorabilia from throughout the state.

Las Cruces co-sponsored a Historic Buildings Survey in 1982, which led to the 1985 inclusion of the two historic development areas of the city on the National Register of Historic Places. The Mesquite Street Original Townsite Historic District is the oldest neighborhood in Las Cruces, containing Klein Park and forty-four of the original eighty-four blocks surveyed in 1849. A number of buildings in this district were razed during urban renewal. Most of the remaining houses are adobe, and have thick walls, narrow scooped rain spouts (*canales*), and peaked roofs. They generally front directly on narrow streets.

The second oldest district is the Alameda-Depot Historic District, originally intended as a residential buffer or suburb between the *acequia madre*, along Water Street, and the railroad. It surrounds Pioneer Park and south to north basically extends from Amador-Lohman to Picacho. Most homes were built between 1890 and 1930 and many have been preserved in their original state. They exemplify a variety of architectural styles. National Register listing means all buildings located therein must be historically significant, must be at least fifty years old and must be not significantly altered.

As mentioned earlier in this document, private businesses also have assumed responsibility for historic preservation. Examples are the Glenn and Sally Cutter restoration-preservation of the Hiram Hadley house, Pioneer Savings and Trust and attorney Lloyd Bates' preservation and maintenance of the Armijo-Gallagher house and Citizens Bank's conservation of the Amador Hotel and planned extensive displays of Amador artifacts after the current remodeling of its main bank in Loretto Towne Center. Still another example is attorney Angel Saenz's complete renovation of the eighty-five year old house at Amador and Campo, which serves as modern law offices.

Many cultural events and opportunities are offered to contemporary Las Crucens, often in cooperation with New Mexico State University. Included in the musical realm are the NMSU-Las Cruces Symphony Orchestra, the Doña Ana Lyric Opera, the Chamber Ballet Company, the Community Concert Association and several university and community choral groups. As to drama, there are the University's American Southwest Theatre Company, presenting five major productions each season; the Community Theatre, which has offered six amateur productions per season since 1963; and the historic Fountain Theater in Mesilla, showing films offered by the Mesilla Valley Film Society. A rather recent challenging and rewarding opportunity for senior citizens is offered in the New Horizons band for oldsters, who either never have played an instrument or have not played since school days. It was organized by NMSU's Dr. William Clark in 1995 and performs at the Community Band's free concerts, presented five or six times annually.

Residents and visitors alike look forward to annual festivals and fiestas. What no doubt is an incomplete list includes early October's city-sponsored Whole

Enchilada Fiesta, featuring the world's largest enchilada, which has become nationally known. Equally noteworthy, and sponsored by the Doña Ana Arts Council, are April's Main and Las Cruces street fairs, the September Artshop gallery tour and the elaborate and very popular November Renaissance Craftfaire. Other events include the International Mariachi Conference, Ft. Selden Frontier Days, *Cinco de Mayo* and Sixteenth of September Fiestas, Juneteenth Celebrations, the spring Border Book Festival which becomes more prestigious and successful each year, and the Southern New Mexico State Fair.

Regional attractions which also draw both residents and visitors include state parks at Elephant Butte and Caballo Lakes, Leasburg and Percha Dams, the State Monument at historic Ft. Selden, and Bureau of Land Management recreation areas at Dripping Springs-La Cueva and at Aguirre Springs. Especially popular is the White Sands National Monument, 275 square miles of gypsum dunes, which move an average of twenty feet east each year.

Another area cultural historical point of interest is the Pueblo Indian community of Tortugas, south of Las Cruces and adjacent to Mesilla Park. In 1888, Pedro Roybal, a Tigua Indian living in Juarez, petitioned for a land grant at the present site of Tortugas. Once the grant was awarded, Felipe Roybal became *cacique*, (or spiritual leader) of the group moving to Tortugas. When he died, his wife, Francisca Avalos de Roybal assumed the leadership role, the first and one of only two females ever to hold the position. By 1910, the annual Fiesta de Guadalupe was moved from Juarez to Tortugas. In 1914, a non-profit corporation, *Los Indigenes de Nuestra Senora de Guadalupe* , (Parishioners of Our Lady of Guadalupe) was organized and built a church, cemetery and four ceremonial buildings. Each year since, the corporation has, in mid-December, sponsored a three-day celebration honoring Our Lady of Guadalupe. One highlight of the Fiesta is an all day pilgrimage to celebrate mass on the summit of "A" or Tortugas Mountain.

Las Cruces also has been active in the Sister Cities Program, one of more than one thousand U. S. cities, located in all fifty states, and more than 1,700 foreign cities, representing 122 countries, which strive to promote positive international relations. Lerdo, of the state of Torreon, Mexico, became a sister city of Las Cruces in 1989 and Nienburg, Germany, became our second sister city in 1993. The local program now is administered by a non profit foundation. Student and adult cultural exchanges are arranged on a regular basis.

Another volunteer organization which serves community needs is the local branch of Habitat for Humanity. The program involves volunteer financial and labor support to build relatively low cost homes. They are built for local residents who can provide their own labor (sweat equity) on their own and future homes in exchange for low-interest loans. The Local Habitat organization was founded in 1987 and is currently completing its thirtieth home.

Other services provided to Las Crucens include the Roadrunner Transit system, two cable TV systems, nine radio stations and NMSU's NPR and PBS stations. The PBS TV channel is celebrating its twenty-fifth year of on-the-air student training. Postal service is provided by 250 employees at a main post office, a new northeast postal annex and seven postal branches. Robert Dinkel recently was named postmaster.

After years of neglect, one of Doña Ana County's most serious "people" problems in areas surrounding Las Cruces has been the development of unincorporated, unzoned, almost unregulated communities called *colonias*. They result from the practice of subdividing land into very small lots and selling them with little or no provision for paved streets, utilities, or police and fire protection. It appears, however, that assistance is on the way to those areas. In mid-1998, Catholic Bishop Ricardo Ramirez and a group called the Colonias Development Council have asked the U.S. Secretary of Housing and Urban Development for a more than three million dollar "Marshall Plan" to improve the lot of colonia residents. Doña Ana County's Commission also recently increased county funding for the Development Council. Further, the 1998 state legislative session addressed the problem with a subdivision act and provision of state funds to match federal resources for improving wastewater facilities. It must be admitted that substandard housing is low-cost housing and that it is in demand because various demographic circumstances have for years kept per capita income in New Mexico and in Las Cruces below national averages. Also, the per capita figure for Las Cruces has been steadily rising with the most recent figure revealing an average per person income of $14, 529.

Population growth and ongoing infra-structure upgrades portend well for the future of Las Cruces. Within the last eighteen months, three new supermarkets, eight new hotels, two new apartment complexes, an Alzheimer's care facility, a twelve screen theater and a senior living complex all have been built. New home building continues on all the city's perimeters and the average cost of an existing three bedroom home is just under $100,000.

With growth, city traffic seems to become heavier almost daily. With the opening of the 600,000 square foot, 90 store Mesilla Valley Mall in 1981, the greatest congestion has shifted in recent years from the Idaho-El

❋ Fabulous Future ❋

Paseo intersection to the Telshor-Lohman intersection, and still more recently to the Elks Drive and Del Rey intersections with North Main. Those intersections carry weekday loads of nearly 50,000 vehicles. Major street improvement plans include an eastward extension of Lohman Avenue to Roadrunner, Interstate 25 underpasses at Stewart and Spruce Streets and multi-million dollar improvements of North Main-Highway 70. Bypass routes also periodically are suggested, including one looping north from Organ around to I -10 West and another angling southwest from Organ to Mesquite.

Statistical measures of economic activity also reflect growth. Gross receipts for the first quarter of 1998 totalled $488 million for Las Cruces and $626 million for Doña Ana County. In each case, this represented between a five and six percent increase over last year. Gross receipts from retail trade alone increased over eleven percent in Las Cruces, rising to $221 million. Commercial construction value also is booming. Building in 1997 totalled almost $40 million, a nearly eight-fold increase over 1993. The June, 1998, commercial permit value jumped twenty-three percent over June, 1997.

Las Cruces' total city budget for this fiscal year is just over $100 million, with projected funding of over $5 million for street projects, over $4 million for flood control and over $2 million for capital projects involving the airport, parks, museums and landscaping. The city also is seeking voter approval of a bond issue to finance improved flood control, major artery street improvement and further efforts to improve disability access to city facilities. The University of New Mexico Bureau of Business and Economic Research predicts that the population of Doña Ana County will rise from its 135, 510 figure in 1990 to 183,602 in 2000 . The Bureau also predicts that the percentage of Hispanics in the county will increase from 50.4% in 1990 to 60.9% in 2000. Its projection for Las Cruces is less optimistic than the 80,000 predictions of local officials, estimating the Las Cruces population will rise from the 1990 figure of 62,126 to at least 74,551 in 2000. All agree, however, that considerable growth will occur. That is, both state and city will "Grow As It Goes."

The history of the City of the Crosses certainly reveals it to have been for one hundred fifty years a significant multi-cultural crossroads and the southern jewel of what truly is the Land of Enchantment. The culmination of those fifteen decades finds the City of the Crosses growing, generally prospering, coping with the demands of growth and the needs of its citizenry, and optimistically looking ahead to a new century in which it will become even more of a major southwestern community.

Of this country's fifty states, New Mexico has demonstrated in its eighty-six years of statehood, a remarkable ability to welcome, accommodate and integrate a populace of multiple backgrounds, ethnicity, and nation of origin. In so doing, it has demonstrated a talent for incorporating a wide range of cultural strengths and abilities into a cosmopolitan whole. Evidence of that multi-cultural cooperative state and community building is found in the fact that in its four hundred year history as a colony, territory and state, New Mexico has had 134 governors: sixty under Spanish rule, fifteen under Mexican rule, six while under U. S. occupation, twenty-four territorial governors and twenty-nine state governors. Las Cruces is truly a multicultural microcosm of a multicultural state, a city meriting the support and pride of its citizens.

Appendix 1

Doña Ana County Sheriffs (1853- 1998)

John Jones 1853
Samuel G. Bean 1854-1860
Marcial Padilla 1861
John Roberts 1862
Fabian Gonzales 1863-1865
Apolonio Barela 1865-1867
Mariano Barela 1867-1871
Thomas Bull 1871-1873
Guadalupe Ascarate 1875-1877
James Southwick 1877-1879
Henry Cuniffe 1879-1882
Eugene Van Patten 1883-1887
Santiago Ascarate 1887-1891
Martin Lohman 1892-1895
Numa Reymond 1896
Pat Garrett 1897-1900
Jose Lucero . . . . .1901-1904; 1909 - 1912; 1917-1920;
. . . . .1925-1928; 1935-36
Felipe Lucero 1905-1908; 1913-1916; 1921-1922;
. 1929-1930
Donaciano Rodriguez 1923-1924
Ricardo Triviz 1931-1934
Mike Apodaca 1941-1943
Santos Ramirez 1944-1948
A.C. Apodaca 1949
Jose Viramontes 1937-1940; 1950-1953;
Frank Romero 1954-1959
Alfredo Garcia 1959-1962
Reyes Barela 1963-1965
Rudolfo Gonzales 1965-1970
Antonio Gonzales 1975-1978
Eddie Dimatteo 1971-1974; 1979-1982
Henry Diaz 1983-1986
Cooney Sarracino 1987-1990
Ray Storment 1990-1994
Jan Cary . . . . .1995 -1998
James Robles . . . . .1998 -

Appendix 2

The following men have served as mayors of Las Cruces since it was incorporated as a town in 1907, based on the Mayor's Gallery in the Council Chambers at City Hall:

Martin Lohman 1907-1908
R. L. Young 1908-1912
J. P. Mitchel 1912-1913
Edward C. Wade, Sr. 1913-1914
R. P. Porter 1914-1916
John H. May 1916-1918
A. I. Kelso 1918-1920; 1922-1924; 1926-1929
J. H. Paxton 1920-1922
Gus Manassee 1924-1926
Vil Lane 1929-1930
T. C. Sexton 1930-1932
Sam Klein   1932-1934; 1938-1944; 1946-1948;
                                   1949-1953
J. Benson Newell 1934-1936
George Frenger 1936-1938
Edwin L. Mechem 1944-1946
James D. McElhannon 1948-1949
Mike F. Apodaca 1953-1955
James F. Neleigh 1955-1961
Edward R. Gutierrez 1961-1962
Edward O. Noble 1962-1963
Thomas J. Graham 1963-1974
Robert Munson 1974-1976
Albert N. Johnson 1976-1980
Joseph A. Camunez 1980-1982
David M. Steinborn 1982-1987
Herculano Ferralez 1987-1989
Tommy Tomlin 1989-1991
Ruben A. Smith 1991-present

Appendix 3

Las Cruces Population Statistics
(U, S. Census, except 1849)

Year	Population	Average Annual Gain	Mesilla
1849	120		3,000 (?)
1850	600	480.0	
1860	768	16.8	2,420
1870	1,240	47.2	1,578
1880	1,685	44.5	
1890	2,340	65.5	1.349
1900	2,906	56.6	1,274
1910	3,836	93.0	1,025
1920	3,969	13.3	1,011
1930	5,811	184.2	1,600
1940	8,385	257.4	
1950	12,325	394.0**	1,264
1960	29,367	1,704.2**	1,269
1970	37,587	822.0	
1980	49,902	1,231.5	
1990	62,126	1,222.4	2,019

** 1950-1960 was the decade of greatest annual growth

Appendix 4

New Mexico State University Enrollment
(Based on Head Count)

Decade	Range	Year of Highest Count
1890-99	23-63	1898
1900-09	32-103	1907
1910-19	56-159	1918
1920-29	142-422	1929
1930-39	455-1171	1939
1940-49	201-1697	1947
1950-59	1303-2862	1959
1960-69	3315-7608	1969
1970-79	8115-11,864	1979
1980-89	12,347-14,300	1989
1990-98	14,809-15,788	1993

Headcount Landmark Years

1. Passed 100 - 1907
2. Passed 200 - 1924
3. Passed 300 - 1927
4. Passed 1,000-1938
5. Passed 10,000 - 1973

Appendix 5

The public drawing of lots subsequent to Lieutenant Sackett's survey of the original Las Cruces town site occurred in 1849. However, it was not until the formalities of establishing and staffing Doña Ana County offices that the plat could be officially recorded. On Sept. 15, 1853, County Clerk P. H. Tucker placed the following in country records:

"I, P. H. Tucker, clerk of the Probate Court in the county of Doña Ana and Territory of New Mexico hereby certify that the written plat of the Town of Las Cruces in said County and Territory was filed in my office on the 15th day of September, A. D. 1853 and that the filing hereof together with the clerk's certificate with the seal of said court attached is duly recorded in my office."

The plat map extended thirteen blocks north to south, from what now are Lohman to Piñon Streets and six blocks east to west, from Tornillo to Water, plus eight blocks south of Lohman. The total plat involved eighty four blocks plus the two blocks for the cemetery and the plaza/church. Deterioration of the 145 year old map prevent an accurate listing of all Las Cruces' charter land owners, but as nearly as they can be deciphered, the following are the names:

Acona	Aldarete	Alvarez	Apodaca	Apple	Armijo
Avalos	Baldonado	Barela	Barrio	Bean	Benavides
Bernadet	Bernal	Bull	Calderon	Campbell	Caponara
Carillo	Churrton	Colman	Constanti	Cordova	Cuniffe
Daguerre	Davis(Duvis?)		Dexter	Durun(Duran?)	
Flotte	Flores	Frigarro	Gallegos	Jones	Lama
Lara	Lewis	Lorenz	Lucas	Lucero	Lujan
Madrid	Maldonado	Marshall	Medina	Miller	Minjares
Montano	Montoya	Ochoa	Olguin	Ortiz	Padilla
Patton	Poles	Reed	Robinson	Samaniego	Sanchez
Sand	Sedillo	Sementa	Serna	Soula	Sostines
Torres	Trujillo	Tucker	Vaca	Valencia	Watts
Woodhouse		Zoeller			

Appendix 6

Presidents of
New Mexico State University

Hiram Hadley	1888 - 1894
Samuel P. McCrea	1894 - 1896
Cornelius Jordan	1896 - 1899
Frederic W. Sanders	1899 - 1901
Luther Foster	1901 - 1908
Winfred Garrison	1908 - 1913
George E. Ladd	1913 - 1917
Austin D. Crile	1917 - 1920
Robert Clothier	1920 - 1921
Harry L. Kent	1921 - 1935
Hugh Gardner	1935 - 1936
Ray Fife	1936 -1938
Hugh H. Milton	1938 - 1947
John R. Nichols	1947 - 1949
John Branson	1949 - 1955
Roger B. Corbett	1955 - 1970
Gerald W. Thomas	1970 - 1984
James E. Halligan	1984 - 1994
James Orenduff	1995 - 1997
William Conroy	1997 -

Appendix 7

Las Cruces area members of Company A, 1st New Mexico Infantry, New Mexico National Guard - Sent to Columbus, NM, Duty, June, 1916

Captain . . . . .Phillip C. Dessauer
1st Lieutenant . . . . .Joe Romero
1st Sergeant . . . . .Tom Roble
Quartermaster Sgt. . . . . . .Demetrio C. Chaves
Sergeants   Juan Gonzales
                      Albino Costales
                      Marin Benavides
Corporales . . . . .Juan Madrid
                      Alejandro Triviz
                      George Woods
                      Frank H. Sanchez
                      Antonio Rodriguez
Cooks . . . . .Frank Brito
                      George Gamboa
Musicians . . . . .Elmer Lohman
                      Willie B. Sierra

Privates

Luis Alvarez	Emilie De La O	Juan Jill
Chon Alvarez	Alfred Flores	Jose Lucero
Rafael Apodaca	Miguel Flores	Manuel Mendoza
Diego Banegas	Marcial Flores	Ambrosio Montoya
Antonio Barncastle, Jr.	Melquiades Flores	Nestor Ortega
Manuel Bernal	Henry Fitch	Gabriel Provencio
Simon Bocan	Edward A. Fountain	Daniel Rivera
Aron Bernal	Edward J. Fountain	Alfonso Romero
Victoriano Cisneros	Heraldo Garcia	Guillermo Treviz
Santiago Cisneros	Elias Garcia	Victorianno
Pedro Cenicero	Roberto Garcia	Villagran
Edward Duran	Sam Geck	Juan Wilson
	Rafael Herrera	

Appendix 8

Doña Ana County World War II Philippines Fatalities
(Corregidor, Bataan, Death March and Labor Camps)
Source: *It Tolled For New Mexico* by Eva Jane Matson

Las Cruces

> Pvt. Auben E. Armstrong
> T5 George W. Cree
> Pvt. Miguel Fierro
> PFC Dionicio R. Peña
> Sgt. Jessie D. Sandell
> Pvt. Marvin R. Sheriff
> PFC Bobby B. Compton
> PFC Almon E. Jackson
> Cpl. John R. McCorkle
> Capt. Charles R. Sparks

Mesilla

> Mr. Thomas H. Casad

Mesilla Park

> Pvt. Francisco Contreras
> Sgt. Leonard Houston
> Pvt. Santiago Mc. Osuna

Doña Ana

> T4 Damacio C. Espalin, Jr.
> Pvt. Andres E. Gloria

La Mesa

> Pvt. Jack A. Parrish

Appendix 9

Hall of Fame Honorees
Doña Ana County Historical Society

1967   Elizabeth Fountain Armendariz
1968   Herbert Yeo
1969   Hugh Milton
1970   Helen Cathey
1971   George Adlai Feather
1972   Katherine Stoes
1973   Fabian Garcia
1974   William and Minnie Newberry Sutherland
1975   Hunter "Preacher" and Edith Lewis
1976   Louis Freudenthal
1977   Opal Lee Priestley
1978   Harriet McGuire and Edmund and Eileen Shannon
1979   Keith Humphreys and the Day sisters, Ruth Lisle, Hester
        Roach and Grace Chance
1980   Ira Clark
1981   Eva Henderson and Margaret Page Hood
1982   The Cox Families
        Carmen Freudenthal
1983   Mary Taylor
1984   No award
1985   Herman Weisner
1986   Ilka Minter
1987   Cal Traylor
1988   Leon Metz
1989   Lee and Christine Myers
1990   Michael Taylor
1991   Pat Beckett
1992   Louis Sadler
1993   Bradley Blake
1994   Jesse Scroggs
1995   Alice Gruver
1996   Gerald Thomas
1997   Bill Stephens
1998   Archie Beckett

Sources

Bartlett, John R., *Personal Narraative of Explorations and Incidents in Texas, New Mexico, California, Sonora and Chihuahua. Vol.1,* Chicago: Rio Grande Press, 1965.

Beckett, Patrick H. and Terry L. Corbett, *The Manso Indians.* Monograph #9, Las Cruces, NM: Coas Publishing, 1992.

Bethune, Martha F., *Race With the Wind: The Personal Life of Albert B. Fall.* El Paso, TX: Privately published, 1989.

Billington, Monroe L., *New Mexico's Buffalo Soldiers.* Niwot, Colorado: University Press of Colorado, 1991.

Boehm, William B., *From Barren Desert To Thriving Community: A Social History of White Sands Missile Range, 1945-1954.* Tularosa, NM: Human Systems Research Inc.(HSR Project #9531), 1997.

Bowden, J. J., *Spanish and Mexican Land Grants in the Chihuahuan Acquisition.* El Paso, TX: Texas Western Press, 1971.

Braden, Jean J., *Mesilla Valley: A Short History* . Las Cruces, NM: Roseta Press, 1982.

Buchanan, Rosemary, *The First Hundred Years.* Las Cruces, NM: Bronson Printing, 1961.

Carmony, Neil B. (ed.), *The Civil War in Apacheland.* Silver City, NM: High Lonesome Books, 1996.

Ellis, Richard N. , *New Mexico Historic Documents.* Albuquerque, NM: University of New Mexico Press, 1975.

Fritz, Scott, *Mesilla Valley Merchants, 1870-1881.* Unpublished M. A. Thesis, Las Cruces, NM: New Mexico State University, 1997.

Garcia, Mary Jane, *An Ethno-History of Doña Ana Village* . Unpublished M. A.. Thesis, Las Cruces, NM: New Mexico

State University, 1986.

Gibson, Arrel M. *The Life and Death of Colonel Albert Jennings Fountain*. Norman, OK: University of Oklahoma Press, 1965.

Griggs, George, *History of the Mesilla Valley*. Las Cruces, NM: Bronson Printing, 1930.

Hall, Dawn, ed., *Drawing the Borderline: Artist-Explorers of the U.S.-Mexico Boundary Survey*. Albuquerque, NM: The Albuquerque Museum, 1996.

Harris, Linda G., *Las Cruces: An Illustrated History* . Las Cruces, NM: Arroyo Press, 1993.

Horgan, Paul, *Great River: The Rio Grande in North American History,* Austin, TX: Texas Monthly Press, 1984.

Jones, Fayette, *Old Mining Camps of New Mexico, 1854-1904* . Santa Fe, NM: Stagecoach Press, 1964.

Kropp, Simon F. *That All May Learn: NMSU 1888-1964*. Las Cruces, NM: New Mexico State University, 1972.

Magoffin, Susan Shelby, *Down the Santa Fe Trail and Into Mexico; the Diary of Susan Shelby Magoffin, 1846-1847*. edited by Stella M. Drumm. New Haven, CT: Yale University Press, 1926.

Matson, Eva J., *It Tolled For New Mexico: New Mexicans Captured By the Japanese 1941-1945*. Las Cruces, NM: Yucca Tree Press, 1994.

McMahon, Iona E. and Eva J. Matson, *A History of the Methodist Church in Las Cruces, 1875 - 1980*. Privately published, no date.

Metz, Leon, *Southern New Mexico Empire: The First National BAnk of Doña Ana County.* El Paso, TX: Mangan Books, 1991.

Miller, Darlis, *The California Column in New Mexico*. Albuquerque, NM: University of New Mexico Press, 1982.

Milton, Hugh, *El Molino-1849*. Doña Ana County Bicentennial Commission-1976.

Neilson, John C. *Communidad: Community Life in a Southwest Town.: Las Cruces, NM 1880-1890*, Unpublished M. A. Thesis, Las Cruces, NM: New Mexico State University, 1988.

Owen, Gordon R., *The Two Alberts: Fountain and Fall*. Las Cruces, New Mexico: Yucca Tree Press, 1996.

Pearce, T. M., *New Mexico Place Names: A Geograhic Dictionary*, Albuquerque, NM: University of New Mexico Press, 1965.

Price, Paxton P., *Mesilla Valley Pioneers, 1823 - 1912,*. Las Cruces, NM: Yucca Tree Press, 1995.

Priestley, Opal L., *Shalam: Utopiaon the Rio Grande 1881-1907*. El Paso, TX: Texas Western Press, 1988.

_____, *Journeys of Faith: The Story of Preacher and Edith Lewis*. Las Cruces, NM: Arroyo Press, 1992.

Rader, Paul, *A History of Western Bank*. Privately published, 1983

Richardson, Barbara J. *Outstanding New Mexico Black Mentors: Past and Present*. Las Cruces, NM: NMSU Black Studies Program 1991.

Sandoval, Raymond E., *Intrusion and Domination: A Study of the Relationship of Chicano Development to the Exercise and Distribution of Power In a Southwestern Community, 1870-1974*. Unpublished Ph.D. Dissertation, University of Washington, 1980.

Simmmons, Marc, *New Mexico: A History*. New York: W. W. Norton, 1977.

Sonnichsen, C.L., *Tularosa: Last of the Frontier West*. Albuquerque: University of New Mexico Press, 1960.

Steeb, Mary, Michael T. Taylor and Anthony Pennock. *Las Cruces Historic Building Survey*. Las Cruces, NM: Doña Ana County Historical Society.

Trumbo. Theron M., *The History of Las Cruces and the Mesilla Valley*. Las Cruces, NM: Historical Data Committee of the Centennial, 1949.

Weisner, Herman B., *The Politics of Justice: A. B. Fall and the Teapot Dome Scandal: A New Perspective*. Albuquerque, NM: Creativer Designs, Inc.,1988.

Newspapers

El Paso Times
Las Cruces Sun News
Las Cruces Bulletin
Las Cruces Citizen
Rio Grande Republican
Thirty Four
Mesilla Valley Independent
Mesilla Valley Democrat

Credits

All photos are from Rio Grande Historical Collections, New Mexico State University Library (Linda Blazer and Tim Blevins) and the personal collection of Margaret Favrot

Index

A

Acoma Pueblo, 3, 10.

Aden Crater, 2.

Alameda-Depot Historic District, 217.

Alameda Hospital (Ranch Resort), 68, 140, 199.

Alamogordo Army Air Base and Bombing Range, 182.

Albuquerque, 7, 16, 18, 40, 41, 48-50, 88, 117.

Amador Hall, 88.

Amador Hotel, 54, 57, 137, 146, 147, 161, 218.

Amador, Martin, 54, 56, 72, 73, 98, 122.

Anza, Don Juan Bautista de, 16.

Apaches, 15, 16, 19, 20, 28, 43, 56, 66, 96, 97, 152.155.

Apache Pass, Battle of, 41.

Apodaca, Sheriff A. L. "Happy", 179.

Aragon, J. J., 142.

Arcadian Club, 63.

Archer, Frank, 132.

Archers, Walter, Ben and Julius, 132, 145.

Armendariz, Elizabeth Fountain, 169.

Armijo-Gallagher House, 146, 155,-157, 218.

Armijo, Isidoro, 50, 118, 207.

Armijo, Jacinto, 54, 72, 157.

Armijo, Gov. Manuel, 18, 31.

Armijo, Nestor, 155, 156.

Art Galleries, 215.

Ascarate, Emilia, 64.

Ascarate, Guadalupe, 72, 99.

Ascarate, Santiago, P. 119.

Atchison, Topeka and Santa Fe Railroad, 49, 50, 51, 121, 133, 154, 157, 213, 215.

Automobiles, 52, 53, 154.

Ayeta, Fr. Francisco de, 13.

B

Baca, Elmo, 197.

Barker, Francis C., 131.

Barker, Percy W. , 131, 145, 166.

Barncastle, John, 45, 46, 54, 155.

Barncastle, Josefa Melendres, 47.

Bartlett, John Russell, 35.

Bataan Death March, 176, 177.

Baylor, Col. John Robert, 38, 39, 61, 150.

Beckett, Archie and Patrick, 152.

Beckett, Isabel Lucero, 151.

Becknell, William, 17, 18.

Bennett, Joseph, 46.

Beltran, Fr. Bernardino, 6.

Bernal, Jose, 20.

Berrier, Edith, 172.

Biedron, Joe, 206.

Billington, Monroe, 217.

Black, Robert, 88.

Block, Harry, 114.

Bond, Ira, 61.

Bonney, William "Billy the Kid", 97.

Bonilla, Francisco Leyva de, 7.

Booker T. Washington School, 151, 171, 208.

Bosque Redondo, 43, 100.

Bowman Bank, 138, 140.

Bowman, Carrie, 63.

Bowman, George D., 137.

Bowman, George R., 54, 80, 85, 137, 138.

Bowman, Henry D., 125, 137, 138.

Bowman, John B., 122, 123.

Boyd, Dr. Nathan, 123, 124, 126, 138-140, 198.

Boyer, Frank, 150, 151.

Branigan, Alice Montgomery, 64, 65, 158.

Branigan Cultural Center, 158, 175, 196, 212.

Branigan Memorial Library, 65, 158, 173, 216.
Branigan, Capt. Thomas, 104, 120, 157, 158, 207.
Brazel, Wayne, 110.
Brazito, 12, 19, 24, 131, 150.
Bull, Thomas, 42, 54, 132.
Butterfield Overland Mail, 36.

C

Caballo Dam, 126.
Caffey, Helen, 169.
California Column, 41, 44-47, 82, 100.
Camino Real, xii, 9, 11, 15, 18, 31, 34, 43,
Canutillo, 6, 12.
Campbell, Patterson Fitzgerald, 144, 145, 166.
Campbell, Judge Richard, 30.
Canby, Col. Edward R. S., 39, 40,
Carleton, Col./Gen. James H., 40-43, 149.
Carson, Col. Christoher "Kit", 43, 149.
Carty, Mother Superior Praxedes, 75-78.
Casad, Thomas, 71, 80, 130, 164.
Casey, Edwin E., 111, 113.
Catron, Sen. Thomas Benton, 109, 117.
Central School, 207.
Chalk Hill, 107.
Chamuscado, Francisco Sanchez, 6.
Chihuahua, 11, 12, 17, 18, 24, 34.
Chivington, Maj./Rev. John, 40.
Citizens Bank, 57, 146, 147, 156, 197, 218.
City Hall Lions, 162.
City Recreation Parks, 209, 210.
Civil War (U. S. War of the Rebellion), 36, 37, 59.
Civilian Conservation Corps, 153, 175.
Clough, Gen. John P., 46.
Coas Book Store, 152, 196.
Colonias, 220, 221.
Comanches, 16.
Compromise of 1850, 35, 36.
Confederate Army, 37-42.
Confederate States of America, 37.
Coogler, Ovida "Cricket", 179, 180.
Corbett, Dr. Roger B., 189, 190, 192.
Cornerstone Campaign for Excellence, 190.
Coronado, Gov. Francisco Vasques de, 5, 6, 10.

Cortez, Fernando, 6, 8.
Costales, Don Jose Maria, 19-21.
Court Junior High, 1941, 208.
Court Youth Center, 58, 208.
Cox, W. W., 110, 120, 131, 140.
Credit Unions, 148.
Crouch, John, 45, 46, 61.
C. S. L. Club, 83.
Cultural Activities, 211, 212, 218.
Cuniffe, Henry, 49, 72, 157.
Cuniffe, Michael, 56.
Curry, Gov. George, 111.
Cutter, Glenn and Sally, 93, 217.

D

Daily, Bradford and Marriocita, 155.
Danburg, Walter M., 118.
Daughenbaugh, Abraham, 138, 139.
Davies, Benjamin E., 45, 46, 131.
Daviet, Dr. L. L., 200.
Davis, Sen./Pres. Jefferson, 35, 37, 38.
Davisson, Emma, 63.
Dawson, Emma, 63, 64.
Dessauer, William, 56, 61, 72, 98.
Doña Ana, 12, 19, 21, 23, 25, 27, 28, 34, 54, 62, 63, 155.
Doña Ana County, 53, 58, 70, 71, 73, 83, 96, 101, 108, 112, 122, 127, 152.
Doña Ana County Commission, 54.
Doña Ana County Court Houses, 57, 98, 175.
Doña Ana County Seat, 53, 101.
Doña County Historical Society, 152, 153, 216.
Doña Ana *paraje*, 19.
Don Bernardo Hotel, 57, 119, 153, 170.
Doniphan, Col. Alexander, 23, 24, 150.
Downtown Mall, 146, 195, 196.
Dripping Springs, 54, 67, 123, 161, 198.
Dwyer, Don and Marie, 93.

E

Early churches, 80, 81, 82.
Elephant Butte Dam, ix, 124, 125, 129, 132, 135, 166, 175.
Elephant Butte Irrigation District (EBID), 121, 125, 126, 128, 130, 214, 215.
Elkins, Stephen B. (Burrows, Julius),113.
El Paso, 9, 13, 14, 15, 18, 20, 38, 40, 100, 101.

Emerick, Sarah and Lewis, 79, 146.
Espejo, Antonio de, 6, 7.
Estevanico, 4.
Evans Brothers (D. M. and J. M.)
Bank, 137.
Evans, Dr. Leland, 199.

F

Fall, Sen./Judge Albert Bacon, 60, 61,
75, 87, 90, 102-106, 108-114, 116, 117,
124, 134, 135, 138, 149.
Farm and Ranch Heritage Museum,
213, 214.
Farmers and Craft Market, 197, 212.
Feather, George Adlai, 79, 153, 171, 172.
Fielder, Clarence, 170.
Fielder, Gertrude, 170, 171, 219.
Fiestas and Festivals, 218, 219.
First National (Security) Bank, 132,
133, 138-144, 146, 147, 162, 194.
First National Tower, 146, 194.
Folk Art, 216.
Fort Bliss, 38.
Fort Fillmore, 27, 33, 38, 39, 41, 42, 55.
Fillmore, Pres. Millard, 35, 59.
Fort Selden, 43, 44, 56, 123, 149.
Fountain, Albert Jennings, 41, 45, 46,
48, 58, 59, 61,65, 69, 71, 74, 82, 83, 85,
87, 88, 90, 97, 98, 100-103,105-107, 109,
110, 114, 130, 139, 149, 170.
Fountain, Henry, 106-108.
Fountain, Mariana Perez, 47, 74, 100,
170.
Frenger, Numa, 111.
Freudental, Carmen, 154.
Freudentahl, Julius, 55, 152.
Freudentahl, Louis, 57, 153, 154.
Frreudenthal, Morris, 153.
Freudenthal, Phoebus, 138, 153.
Freudenthal, Mrs. Phoebus, 64.
Freudenthal, Samuel, 54.
Fry, R. H., 119.

G

Gadsden, James, 35.
Gadsden Purchase, 35, 38, 49, 152.
Galles, Nicholas, 127, 139.
Garcia, Fabian, 91, 164, 165.
Gardiner, Prof. Anna, 186.
Gardiner, Prof. George W., 185, 186,
191, 192.
Garrett, Elizabeth, 110.

Garrett, Patrick Floyd, 97, 107, 108,
109, 110, 111, 152.
Garrison, Pres. Winfred , 78.
Geck, Jessie, 71.
Geck, Louis, 42.
Gilliland, Jim, 108.
G. I. Bill, 191.
Glorieta, Battle of, 40, 41.
Goddard Hill, 191.
Goddard, Ralph Willis, 180, 181.
Goddard, Robert Hutchings, 180, 181,
183.
Gonzales, Supt. Jesse, 208.
Gonzales, Jose, 207.
Gran Quivira, 5, 12.
Grand Army of the Republic, Phil
Sheridan Post #14, 82.
Greater Las Cruces Chamber of
Commerce, 144, 206.
Gregg, Josiah, 18.
Guadalupe Hidalgo, Treaty of, 25, 34,
35.

H

Habitat for Humanity, 220.
Hadley Hall, 94, 190.
Hadley, Pres. Hiram, 84, 85, 87-89, 92,
93, 124, 165, 217.
Hadley, Katharine, 63.
Haines, Ben, 142.
Haner, Charles, 142.
Harper, Justin, 146.
Harwood, Rev. Thomas, 80.
Hernandez, Arnulfo "Nufie", 206.
Hidalgo y Costilla, Fr. Miguel, 17.
Hillsboro, 108, 139.
Hispaño Chamber of Commerce, 206,.
Holloman Air Base, 183, 184, 205.
Holt, Alfred Moss, 91.
Holt, Herbert B., 125, 134, 140, 141.
Hoover, Austin, 217.
Howland, Andrew, 62, 63.
Humaña, Antonio Gutierrez de, 7.

I

Independent Democrat, 61.
Ikard, J. A. , 145, 146.
Ikard, James, 145, 146.
Ikard, John, 145, 146.
Immaculate Heart of Mary Cathedral,
78.

J

Johnson, Dallas, 145.
Johnson Test Facility (NASA), 188,.
Jordan, Pres. Cornelius, 92.
Jornada del Muerto, 9,12.
Jornada and El Paso Reservoir and Canal Co., , 122. (John B. Bowman and Simon B. Newman)
Juarez (El Paso del Norte) 4, 13, 19, 184.

K

Kearny, Col. Stephen Watts, 22, 23, 82.
Kelley, Robert, 61.
Kelso, A. I., 141, 142.
Kilbourne Hole, 2.
King Philip II, 7.
Kinney, John, 97, 98.
Klein, Mayor Samuel, 173, 177, 200.
Korean War, 187.

L

La Esquina, 196.
LaPoint, Lawrence, 45, 54, 72.
LaPoint, Candelaria Lucero, 47.
Larkin, Ralph Roy, 91.
Las Cruces Centennial, 177, 178.
Las Cruces College, 86.
Las Cruces Drama and Muscial Club, 66.
Las Cruces Founding, 28-30.
Las Cruces High School, 1956, 208.
Las Cruces, Incorporation as a Town, 119.
Las Cruces Town Company, 49, 50.
Lassaigne, Fr. Pedro, 75, 77.
Lee, Oliver M., 104, 108.
Legislature, State, 144.
Legislature, Territorial, 103, 114.
Lemon, John, 44, 56, 149, 150.
Lesinsky, Charles, 54.
Lesinsky, Henry, 54, 55, 72, 133, 152.
Lesinsky, Morris, 131.
Lewis, Rev. Hunter "Preacher", 81.
Lincoln County, 95, 96.
Llewellyn, Morgan, 111.
Llewellyn, William H. H. 73, 104, 111, 114, 157, 158.
Lohman, Fred, 73.
Lohman, Martin, 55, 72, 73, 104, 119, 133.

Loretto Academy, 54, 75, 76, 85, 119, 146, 147, 194.
Loretto Shoppping Mall, 76, 133, 146, 147, 194, 197.
Loretto Towne Centre, 147, 197, 207, 218.
Los Organos (Organ Mountains), 59.
Lost Padre Mine, 59.
Lucero, Barbaro, 122, 152.
Lucero, Estevan, 119.
Lucero, Sheriff Felipe, 120, 134, 152.
Lucero, Sheriff Jose, 152.
Ludwick, Russell and Julia, 93.
Lujan, Geronimo, 20.
Lundeen, Gerald, 196.
Lynde, Maj. Isaac., 38, 39.
Lyon, Carrie, 63.

M

MacArthur, Capt. Arthur, 43.
MacArthur, Douglas, 43, 143.
Maddox, Dr. A. D., 200.
Madonna School, 78, 78, 79.
Magoffin, Susan Shelby, 31.
Manso Indians, 3, 6, 9.
Martin, John, 45, 48.
Masonic Order, Aztec Lodge #3, 82.
May, John A., 72, 73, 135.
Mayfield High School, 1965, 208.
McBride, Dr. Robert E., 67, 120, 121, 198.
McCrea, Pres. Samuel P., 92.
McFie Hall, (Old Main) 89, 91, 190.
McFie, Judge John R., 85, 88, 98.
McFie, Mary, 64.
McFie, Maude, 90.
McFie, Ralph.111.
McGrath, Lemuel C., 91.
McNew, William, 108.
McSain, William P. B., 141.
Melendres, Pablo, 20, 21, 28, 29, 54.
Melendres, Pablo, Jr., 71, 99.
Memorial General Hospital, 200.
Memorial Medical Center, 200.
Memorial Medical Center Health-Plex, 202.
Memorial Medical Center, Incorporated (MMC, Inc.), 201,.
Mendoza, Viceroy Antonio de, 4, 5.
Mescalero Reservation,17, 21, 42, 55, 66, 157, 159.
Mesilla, 26, 27, 28, 33, 36, 38, 41, 42, 44,

48, 49, 52, 53, 54, 59, 65, 72, 80, 99, 101, 102, 147, 152.
Mesilla Dramatic Association, 65.
Mesilla Park, 78, 172.
Mesilla political riot, 1871, 104, 150.
Mesilla Valley, 2, 11, 13, 18, 26, 48, 50, 52, 75,100, 102, 114, 124, 136, 165, 198.
Mesilla Valley Hospice, 202.
Mesilla Valley Hospital, 202.
Mesilla Valley *Independent*, 61.
Mesilla Valley Mall, 197, 221.
Mesquite Street Original Town Site Historic District, 217.
Mexican-American War, 25, 34.
Miller, Charles D., 134.
Mills, Col. Anson, 123, 124.
Milton, Gen. Hugh M., 143, 181, 182.
Modoc Mine, 60.
Mogollon Indians, 3.
Montoya, Barnabe, 20.
Moreno, Presiliano, 119.
Museums, 211, 212.

N

Nakayama, Carl, 166, 168.
Nakayma, Roy and Rose, 165, 166, 167, 168.
Nakayama, Kaichiro "John", 165.
Narvaez, Panfilo de, 4.
Nava, City Manager Jesus, 206.
Navajos, 15, 16, 23, 43, 100.
Newbrough, Dr. John, 62, 63.
Newcomb, Simon B., 49, 61, 69, 71, 72, 83, 98, 99, 122, 157.
New Mexico College of Agriculture and Mechanic Arts, 90, 165, 189.
New Mexico State University, ix, 90, 170, 190, 192,.
Newman, Simon Harry, 61, 71, 72.
Niza, Fr. Marcos de, 5.
Nuestra Señora de las Candelaria Church (Doña Ana), 79.

O

O'Donnell, Academic Vice President William, 192.
Oñate, Don Juan de, 8, 9, 10, 11, 12, 20.
Oñate High School, 1993, 208.
Organ, 59, 110.
Organ Mountains, 1, 9, 34, 155.
Ortiz, Fr. Raymond, 26.
Otermin, Gov. Antonio de, 13, 14.

Otero, Gov. Miguel A., 112, 117.

P

Pan-American Center, 192.
Papen, Frank O., 133, 142, 143, 144, 146, 147, 187.
Park Hotel, 58, 140, 162.
Pennock, Tony, 215.
Pershing, Gen. John J., 134.
Phillips Chapel School, 208.
Physical Science Laboratory (PSL) 164, 185, 191.
Pierce, Pres. Franklin, 35.
Pike, Lt. Zebulon, 16.
Pioneer (City) Park, 58, 65, 209.
Pioneering Artist Colony, 215
Pioneer Savings and Trust and Lloyd Bates, 218.
Polk, Pres. James K., 22.
Pope' (Po-Pay), 13, 14.
Popular Dry Goods, 162, 196.
Porter, Lt. William C., 176.
Priestly, Opal Lee, xiii, 64.
Price, Col. Sterling, 23, 24.
Prince, Judge/Gov. L. Bradford, 50, 89, 90.
Prisoner of War (P.O.W.) Camps, 177.
Pueblo Revolt, 13, 20.

Q

Quesenberry, Capt. Joseph, 135.
Quivira, 10.

R

Railroad arrival, 1881, 50.
Ramirez, Bishop Ricardo, 220.
Reymond, Jettie, 63.
Reymond, Numa, 55, 73, 85, 86, 88, 107, 131, 137, 153.
Reymond, Katie, 64.
Reynolds, A. H., 137.
Reynolds, Guadalupe Ancheta, 47.
Retirement Centers, 211.
Revista Catolica, 74.
Rio Grande, 2, 8, 9, 13, 17, 18, 22-24, 26, 30, 32, 35, 36, 40, 41, 43, 44, 52, 62, 75, 81, 121, 122, 137.
Rio Grande Dam and Irrigation Company, 124.
Rio Grande Historical Collections, 217.
Rio Grande Land Agency (Mesilla Park), 52.

Rio Grande *Republican,* 61.
Roads, highways, 154.
Robertson, William, 145.
Robledo, Ana, 19.
Robledo, Pedro, 9, 19.
Rodriguez, Fr. Augustin, 6.
Rogiere, Padre Doñato, 77
Roosevelt, Theodore, 111, 112, 115, 158, 159.
Ross, Rex, 194.
Roualt, Theodore, 56, 130.
Roualt, Theodore, Jr., 118, 139.
Roybal, Pedro, Felipe and Francisca, 219.
Ruelas, Don Rafael, 26.
Ryan, Monsignor William, 195.
Rynerson, William L, 45, 46, 49, 52, 54, 60, 61, 69, 72, 83, 85, 88, 97, 98, 130, 150, 155, 157, 159.

S

Sackett, Lt. Delos Bennett, 28, 30.
Saenz, Angel, 218.
Saint Genevieve's Church, 29, 42, 56, 75, 77-79,146, 195.
San Albino Church (Mesilla), 27, 79, 150.
Sanders, Pres. Frederic W., 92.
San Juan Pueblo, 9.
Santa Anna, Pres. Antonio Lopez de, 26, 35.
Santa Fe, 9, 11-13, 14, 15, 16, 18, 20, 22, 23, 34, 36, 40, 41, 48, 49, 75, 87, 88, 103.
Santa Fe Trail, 22, 31, 34.
Santa Teresa Port of Entry, 205.
Sattley, James F. and Clyde A., 126, 127, 138, 139.
Schaublin, Jacob, 72, 85, 122, 132, 133.
Schutz, Aaron, 56, 61, 72.
Sedgwick, Drs. James and William, 200.
Senior Citizen Centers, 210.
Senior Services, 211.
Seven Cities of Cibola, 5.
Shalam Colony, 62, 63, 140, 166, 198.
Sibley, Col. and General Henry H., 38, 39, 40, 41.
Sisters Cities Foundation, 219, 220.
Sisters of Loretto, 75.
Sisters of Our Lady of the Good Shepherd, 78, 79.
Smith, C. B. and Josephine, 159, 160, 161, 177, 196.

Smith, Ruben, 161.
Smith, Steven L., CEO, MMC, Inc., 202.
Snow, Oscar C., 90, 91, 125, 130, 140, 141.
Sosa, Gaspar Castaño de, 7.
South Ward School, 72, 73, 87, 207, 209.
Spaceport and Spaceport City, 205.
Spanish flu, 1918, 135.
Spanish-American War, 111,.
Sperry, C. Fay, 139, 140.
Stahmann, Deane, 136.
Stahmann, W. J.,136.
Statehood, 117.
State Parks and Monuments, 219.
Steel, Samuel A., 90, 91.
Stephenson, Horace, 54, 99 .
Stephenson, Hugh, 54, 59, 131.
Stephenson-Bennett Mine, 59, 60.
Stern, E. J. (Gene) and Mable, 161-163.
Stoes, Henry and Katharine, 64, 169.
Sutherland, William A., (Mr. Aggie), 140, 141.
Swartz, Sara, 169.
Swisher, Mary, 171.

T

Taft, Pres.William H., 117, 158.
Taos Pueblo, 3, 22, 31.
Telegraph lines, 1876, 48.
Texas-New Mexico Water Disputes, 214, 215.
Tharp, Claud, 142.
Thirty Four, 61, 72.
Thomas, Pres. Gerald, W., 91, 192, 217.
Tombaugh, Clyde and Patsy, 163, 164.
Topley, Louise, 132, 133.
Tortugas, 13, 54, 67, 160, 219.
Treviño, Juan Francisco, 13.
Trost Architectural Firm, 190, 207.
Trinity Site, 182, 183.

U

Ugarte, Gen. Mauricio, 20.
Union High School, 1925, 207.
University buildings, 190, 191, 192.
University Presidential Residence, 191.
University Research Centers, 193.
Urban Renewal, 194, 195.

V

Vaca, Alvillar Nuñez Cabeza de, 4.

Vado, 150, 151, 161.
Valverde, Battle of, 40.
Van Patten, Col. Eugene, 54, 76, 77, 85, 97, 99, 112, 198.
Van Patten's Hall, 66.
Vargas, Don Diego de, 14.
Victorio, Chief (Apache), 97.
Victorio Peak (the Doc Noss story), 60, 174.
Villa, Col. Pancho, 57, 133, 134, 159.
Von Braun, Dr. Wernher, 183, 185.
V- 2 Rocket, 183-185.

W

Wade, Edward C., 69, 98, 99, 159.
Walker, Lawrence, 145.
Wallace, Gov. Lew, 97.
Ward, C. W., 73.
Water Tank Murals, 215.
Wednesday Literary Club, 63.
Western Bank (Community First), 146, 147.
Whelpley, Earl, 194.
White Sands Proving Ground, 164, 182, 186.
White Sands Missile Range,. 61, 143, 164, 187, 188, 190, 205.
Whitmore, James, 88.
Whole Enchilada Fiesta, 218.
Williams, Clara Belle 170.
Williams, Constable Ben, 105, 106.
Williams, Kate Agnes, 91.
Wolfe, Calla K. Eylar, 168.
WIA Club House, 65.

Women's Improvement Association (WIA), 64, 65, 154, 162, 169, 209.
Woodhull, Capt. Samuel, 140, 141.
Woodworth, Dr. Oscar, 67.
World War I, 135.
World War II, 175-177, 191.
WPA and PWA, 191.

Y

Young, Judge R. L., 85, 119, 191.

Z

Zaldivar, Juan de, 10.
Zuni Pueblo (Hawikuh), 5.